THE OLD HOUSE BOOK OF COTTAGES AND BUNGALOWS

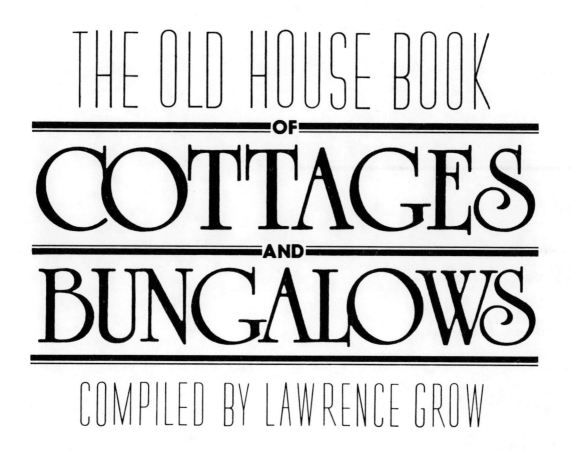

THE OLD HOUSE BOOK OF COTTAGES AND BUNGALOWS

COMPILED BY LAWRENCE GROW

 A Sterling/Main Street Book
Sterling Publishing Co., Inc.   New York

Library of Congress Cataloging-in-Publication Data

Grow, Lawrence.
  The old house book of cottages and bungalows.

  Bibliography: p.
  Includes index.
    1. Cottages—United States—Designs and plans.
  2. Bungalows—United States—Designs and plans.
  I. Title.
  NA7561.G76   1987   728.3'7'0223   87-5481
  ISBN 1-55562-016-7

10 9 8 7 6 5 4 3 2 1

A Sterling / Main Street Book

© 1987 by The Main Street Press
Published by Sterling Publishing Company, Inc.
387 Park Avenue South, New York, N.Y. 10016
Distributed in Canada by Sterling Publishing
% Canadian Manda Group, P.O. Box 920, Station U
Toronto, Ontario, Canada M8Z 5P9
Distributed in Great Britain and Europe by Cassell PLC
Artillery House, Artillery Row, London SW1P 1RT, England
Distributed in Australia by Capricorn Ltd.
P.O. Box 665, Lane Cove, NSW 2066
Manufactured in the United States of America
All rights reserved

ISBN 0-55562-016-7

Contents

Contents

Introduction

In compiling a book of American cottage and bungalow designs from the mid-1800s to the 1930s, there is a great deal of material to choose from. Illustrated in hundreds of popular 19th- and early 20th-century house plan books and periodicals are thousands of possible candidates. Cottages were built of every possible size, shape, and style. What was considered an adequate home for a Hudson Valley farmer of the 1850s, for example, was too ambitious a design for a small-town workingman's family of the same period. In shape, cottages ranged from hillside chalets to rigorously symmetrical New England saltboxes. Although the popular mind continues to think the cottage a simple dwelling meant to house a single family, the style in which a cottage was built varied from decade to decade and usually mirrored the architectural fashions of the time.

The bungalow is almost as difficult a building type to define as the cottage. A development of the late-Victorian period in America, the form is traced to roots in India. There, a one-story house of light construction with verandahs around all four sides and a widely projecting roof was called a bungalow. The classic American bungalow of the early 1900s has a recessed verandah or porch across its front, and a low sloping roof from which a dormer projects. The building may be one or two stories high.

By the 1920s the term "bungalow" was often used interchangeably with "cottage." In popular architectural literature, a bungalow came to mean simply an inexpensive, small dwelling. For the purposes of this book, a bungalow is a type of cottage popular from the early 1900s to the 1930s. The cottage or bungalow is, then, almost by definition, a vernacular or popular building. While it may partake of a particular style in some elements, overall style is secondary to economy or utility. Many of these houses are of only one story and have as few add-ons and amenities as possible. Often built on a small inexpensive lot, the cottage or bungalow may contain as few as three rooms and rarely has more than six. These were homes built to be maintained without servants or daily help.

The cottage and bungalow designs included in this book are almost all houses intended for year-round use, but a few seasonal or vacation buildings from the 1880s and '90s are included. A cottage, whatever its purpose, was rarely given serious attention by high-style architects. While not a frivolous form of architecture, the cottage was considered an informal type of building, certainly worthy of an architect's skill, if not much of his time. A house that might cost $750 in the 1850s or $4,000 in the 1920s was simply not a rewarding candidate for an architect trying to make his reputation. Few cottage dwellers, of course, were even in a position to pay an architect's fee. Instead, during the period surveyed in this book, they turned for inspiration and guidance to house plan books produced by architectural firms and to popular magazines.

Considering the limited attention given this type of building by the architectural profession, it is surprising to find how many of these modest dwellings are well designed. A few leading architects in every period felt it their obligation to improve the state of popular home building and contributed to the raising of aesthetic standards. Deserving much more credit for the achievement of imaginative cottage designs, however, are the little-known architects who translated the work of the high-stylists in a vernacular mode. It was through the circula-tion of their practical house plan books and other printed literature from the mid-1800s until the early 20th century that significant changes were made.

All of the designs included in *The Old House Book of Cottages and Bungalows* are drawn from the popular literature produced by architects. These are the model houses of the past, ready-made plans that cost little to buy and which were inexpensive to execute. When compared with the same type of literature available today in builder's magazines, these now old-fashioned designs take on a new value. Nearly all can be adapted and executed economically and effectively today. And each has charm, a character sadly missing from much of the contemporary building scene.

1.

ROMANTIC RETREATS:
The Early Victorian Cottage

Cottage has a charmingly sweet sound, and is, perhaps more suggestive of comfortable thoughts than any other word in our language, but that of home.

William H. Ranlett, The Architect (1851)

In the 18th century Marie Antoinette kept a humble cottage in which she played peasant. The royal lords of Georgian England retreated from time to time to picturesque abodes deep in the country where they could enjoy nature and live a simple life. Wealthy merchants of colonial New York retired on weekends to rustic cottages up the Hudson far from business and formal social life. A pretty, quaint cottage was considered a fitting and fashionable form of building for informal country living in the late 18th and early 19th centuries. This romantic view of cottage life was expressed in poetry, music, art, and fiction, as well as architecture. The fact that the buildings favored by the privileged might bear little or no resemblance to the humble cottages of the poor was not allowed to disturb the popular pastoral dream.

The architects of the first half of the 19th century who first formally addressed the subject of cottage architecture in America had few illusions about the wretched condition of country life. Men such as William Ranlett, Andrew Jackson Downing, and Calvert Vaux, held firmly, nonetheless, to the European romantic architectural vision expertly summed up in J. C. Loudon's *Encyclopedia of Cottage, Farm, and Villa Architecture and Furniture*, published first in London in 1833 and frequently reprinted in the United States thereafter. Downing and his contemporary Andrew Jackson Davis were the leading proponents of the English Gothic style of rural architecture and crusaded to transform the bleak country landscape. Ranlett, Vaux, Richard Upjohn, and Gervase Wheeler followed in their path with ever more elaborate designs for villas and cottages. Only from time to time did they address the needs of the low-income farmer or mechanic.

To Henry Cleaveland, William Backus, Samuel Backus, and Lewis K. Allen—all architects and authors of house-plan books—we owe the first practical and aesthetically pleasing cottage designs. They, too, were entranced with romantic villas and country estates, but they addressed themselves to more democratic needs. Cleaveland and the Backus brothers spoke for their fellow popularizers in the preface to their *Village and Farm Cottages* (1856):

> The admirable publications of the much lamented Downing gave a new and lasting impulse to the architecture of our country residences. We shall feel rewarded if we may be considered to have done something in the same direction, with regard to a humbler class of structures.

The designs of men such as these represent the majority of those shown in the following pages on early Victorian cottage architecture.

TWO PLAIN COTTAGES.

"The Plain Cottages" illustrated in William Ranlett's *The Architect* (1851) are representative of the rural American laboring class dwelling of the mid-nineteenth century. The average house had little more than four walls, a chimney, and a roof. Windows were small and few; an entry porch or even a stoop was uncommon. Sleeping accommodations were found on the main floor or were provided in a badly lit and aired attic space. Cooking was often performed in a corner of the sitting room and so, too, was eating. As economic conditions im-proved in the succeeding Victorian decades, stylistic and structural improvements were made to the exterior and interior of the average modest cottage. The editors of farm journals increasingly devoted space to advice on how to improve a common dwelling or to inexpensively build a more picturesque cottage. And authors of house plan books, such as Ranlett, prepared more and more volumes. He had his own ideas for dressing up "The Plain Cottages," the plans for which are shown on the following page.

THE SAME ORNAMENTED.

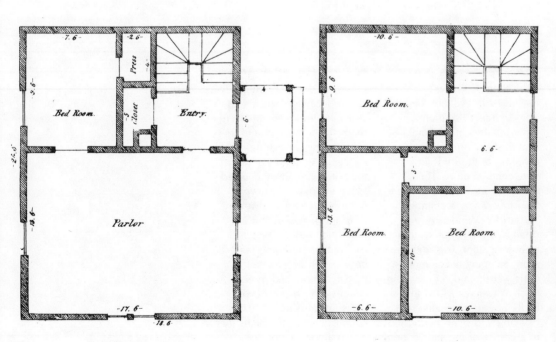

FIRST-FLOOR PLAN.   SECOND-FLOOR PLAN.

Ranlett captioned his drawings of his redesigned plain cottages "The Same Ornamented." The changes, however, are considerable. From the rusticated foundation to the rebuilt chimney, each building has been transformed. The walls appear to be stuccoed, probably for reasons of insulation and aesthetic appearance. Dormers open the second floor to air and light. Windows have been given ornamental caps and the gables possess decorative vergeboards. These are no longer "mean" dwellings but picturesque cottages worthy of any respectable working man and his family. Ranlett notes that both cottages have been built so that they could be transported long distances, there to be properly sited and ornamented.

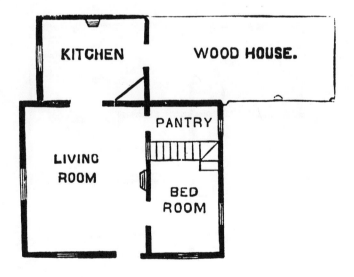

FLOOR PLAN.

The Illustrated Annual Register of Rural Affairs (1855-56) recommended this "laborer's cottage" and claimed that it would cost only $200 to build. The walls are made of unplaned board or rough plank with batten three inches wide nailed over each joint. Architectural distinction is provided by the eave brackets, door cap, and window caps or hoods. "To avoid a flimsy appearance, and give the house a substantial air," the *Register* recommended that "these brackets and caps should be made of plank at least two inches in thickness." In addition to the three rooms on the main floor, space is alloted for two bedrooms on the second floor. The recommended room sizes are not provided, the designer believing that size "may be suited to circumstances."

The design of Lewis K. Allen's cottage is similar to that of the *Annual Register* illustrated on the opposite page. Allen's plan was published in 1851 in *Rural Architecture*, a house plan book. A nearly square space (20' x 16') is joined to a rear rectangle (26' x 8'). There is a garret overhead for sleeping, this space being reached by a swing stepladder. A dormer at the rear provides light and air. The cottage was recommended for a childless couple or a single person. As in the previous design, ample space is given to an area housing the wood supply, this designated "W.H." on the floor plan.

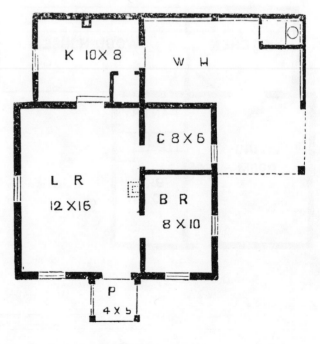

FLOOR PLAN.

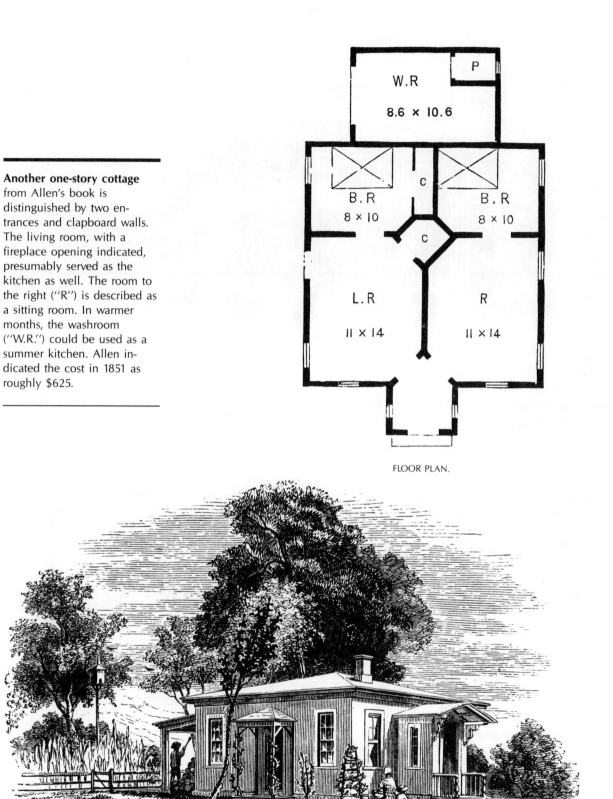

FLOOR PLAN.

Another one-story cottage from Allen's book is distinguished by two entrances and clapboard walls. The living room, with a fireplace opening indicated, presumably served as the kitchen as well. The room to the right ("R") is described as a sitting room. In warmer months, the washroom ("W.R.") could be used as a summer kitchen. Allen indicated the cost in 1851 as roughly $625.

Andrew Jackson Downing first published his plan for a ''Square Farm Cottage'' in his *Horticulturist* during the late 1840s, and it was reproduced in the 1855-56 *Illustrated Annual Register of Rural Affairs.* The house was said to have cost $760 to build and provided such amenities as a trellised front porch, entrance hall, and two chimneys drawn together in the attic. The ground floor rises 10'; the upper, 9'. The overall dimensions are 24' x 30'. At least two of the upstairs bedrooms could be well heated as they are provided with fireplaces, an uncommon touch at the time for such a modest house.

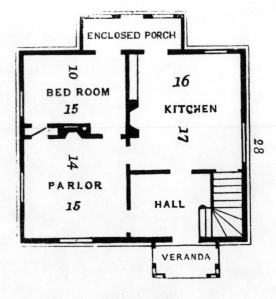

FIRST-FLOOR PLAN.

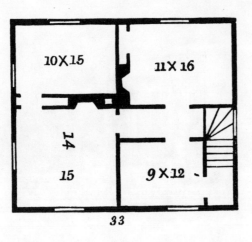

SECOND-FLOOR PLAN.

Similar to many vernacular mid-Victorian cottages is this model from *Village and Farm Cottages* (1856) by Henry W. Cleaveland, William Backus, and Samuel D. Backus. The house was designed for a couple with one child and could be built for $650. In form the building is very regular and, therefore, relatively simple in construction. Because the addition of an attractive verandah, board-and-batten siding, and window hoods of plank strips, the cottage is by no means without visual interest and character.

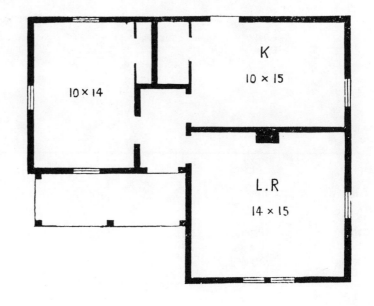

FLOOR PLAN.

18

The simplest cottage design presented by Cleaveland and his two partners in *Village and Farm Cottages* is ''fitted only for a family of the smallest size and most moderate means.'' The cost: $575. The living room is to serve as a kitchen and dining room, as well; the sitting room is the true place of relaxation, but might also be used as a bedroom. The main section measures only 10' x 17'; attached to it is a wood room or shed. The ornamental front porch and the board-and-batten siding add immeasurably to the cottage's attractive appearance. No fireplaces are provided for. In the authors' words: ''The use of stoves is so nearly universal in houses of this class, that there is but little inducement to provide other means for warming or cooking.'' Stove pipes rise from the living room and sitting room to the attic chimney.

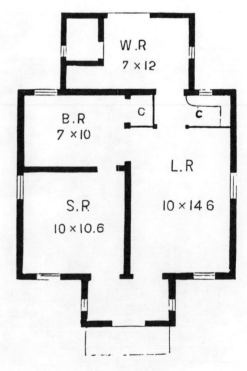

FLOOR PLAN.

Designed as a summer cottage or year-round house for a small family, this plan by Cleaveland, Backus, and Backus is intended to "show more attention to symmetry" and "more care in details" than others of their one-story cottage plans. Verandahs are tucked under the eaves on each side of a wide front entry hall. The main entrance is protected by a broad, bracketed door hood. The cost in 1856 was moderate — $1,000.

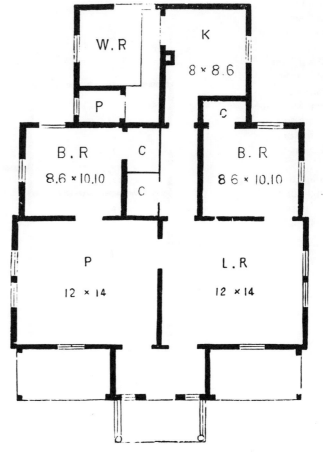

FLOOR PLAN.

This small, one-room deep, story-and-a-half cottage is representative of a modest but stylish mid-nineteenth-century domestic building. Architects Cleaveland, Backus, and Backus attempted to improve on the common square box of the period. Their chief alteration was the placement of a stairway in the center of the house rather than at one of the room ends. In their words, "No room is made the passage way to another room." Additionally, they have provided for a center front hall, thereby eliminating the necessity of an outer door opening directly into the living room or kitchen. The first-floor end windows are tripartite, "improving the outside look, while they make the inside cheerful." The bedroom windows are double size rather than single units. The cost of such an improved two-story house was $820.

FIRST-FLOOR PLAN.

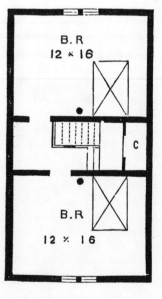

SECOND-FLOOR PLAN.

SECOND-FLOOR PLAN.

FIRST-FLOOR PLAN.

Lewis Allen published his two-story cottage design in *Rural Architecture* (1851) and suggested it was suitable for a farm of 20, 50, or 100 acres. If of frame construction, it cost between $800 and $1,200; if brick or stone, $1,500. The basic design is similar to many early New England houses, a wing at the rear leading to a wagon-house, workshop, piggery, and feed storage room. Such direct communication between house and outbuildings was advantageous during cold winter months. Allen has added several features which are improvements on the earlier New England model, such as a covered porch, center hall, separate kitchen, and two small bedrooms on the first floor. Unlike many other architects of the time, he has not provided for a stove flue in the kitchen but for a full fireplace and bake oven. These two elements, he wrote, are "homely and primitive comforts still dear to many of us who are not ready to concede that all the virtues of the present day are combined in a 'perfection' cooking stove, and a 'patent' heater." The overall dimensions of the main block are 40' x 30'.

Hillside or bank houses were built from the earliest colonial times in America. By the mid-1800s interest in what was termed a "Swiss" or chalet-style dwelling was very much current. A house of this picturesque profile would include balconies, verandahs, brackets at the eaves, and other decorative elements. The building would be pitched on a slope, of course, so as to allow for a working "basement," open on one side, and one or two additional floors. This design from *Village and Farm Cottages* (1856) by Cleaveland, Backus, and Backus, includes a kitchen, vegetable cellar ("v.c."), fuel cellar ("f"), and living room on the lowest level. The basement walls are of stone, and the principal rooms open up at ground level. Board-and-batten siding covers the walls of the upper two stories. The cost of this ambitious and handsome cottage was $1,375.

BASEMENT FLOOR PLAN.

MAIN FLOOR PLAN.

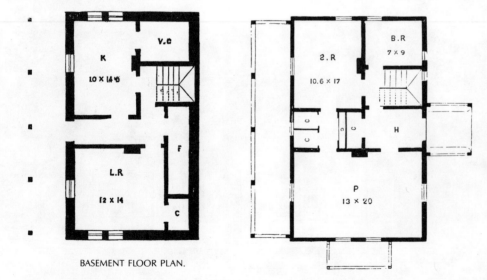

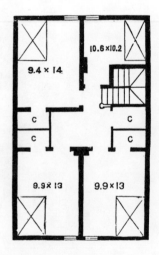

SECOND-FLOOR PLAN.

Clearly designed in imitation of a Swiss chalet, this building features a three-story superstructure which supports a flight of stairs and a gallery. The house is entered from the road on which it fronts. Another Cleaveland, Backus, and Backus design, it is almost square, measuring 23' x 28'. A special feature of the main floor is a large bedroom fitted with a fireplace, a room that could be used "in case of sickness." The lower walls are of stone, and board-and-batten siding is used for the upper levels. A cost of $1,300 was estimated.

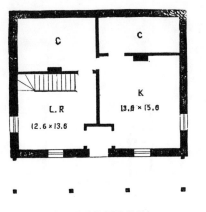

BASEMENT FLOOR PLAN.

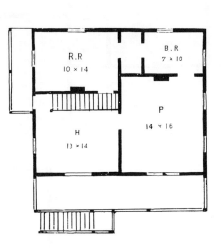

MAIN FLOOR PLAN.

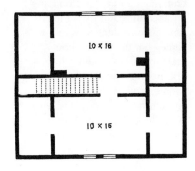

SECOND-FLOOR PLAN.

**Recognizably Victorian
Gothic in form** is the steeply-
pitched two-story cottage
designed by Cleaveland,
Backus, and Backus. The
overall irregularity of form,
bracketed eaves, balcony,
wide verandah, and fancy
chimney cap give the building
an appealing high style for its
time. The designers were
somewhat defensive about
their romantic model: "If he
[the homeowner] prefers the
square, dreary, double house,
so common formerly, his wish
is easily gratified, and for a
model he can take a packing
box."

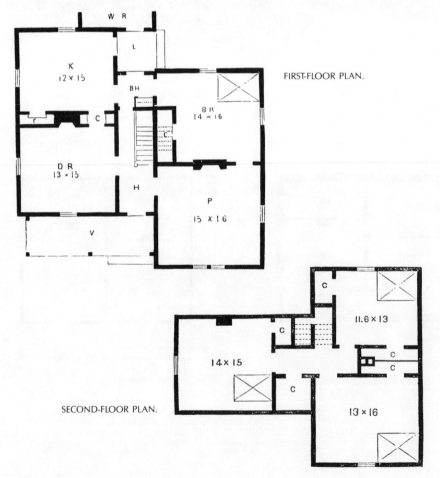

FIRST-FLOOR PLAN.

SECOND-FLOOR PLAN.

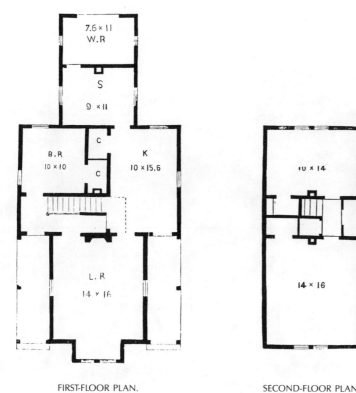

FIRST-FLOOR PLAN.

SECOND-FLOOR PLAN.

It would cost approximately $1,100 to build this delightful cottage, said the architects Cleaveland, Backus, and Backus in 1856. The two-story building is considerably smaller and more compact than the design on the opposite page, but it is just as appealing. Verandahs run along each side of the front living room section; on the front is a square bay window. Entrance to the house may be made through any of the three principal front rooms. The rear wing, the architects suggested, was optional. Rather than using a back or summer kitchen ("S") and wood room ("W.R."), a simple wood shed could be attached. Board-and-batten siding was considered the only appropriate style for the exterior; "clapboards would seriously injure its character."

The very simple but charming cottage illustrated here is the least expensive of the Cleaveland, Backus, and Backus two-story models, costing less than $1,000 in 1856. The architects knew exactly for whom the house was designed: "We may suppose its owner to be moderate in his wishes, and somewhat exact, perhaps, in his habits. With no family but himself and wife, with a small but regular income, he has built according to his taste and means. No idea of future change or extension entered his head. Its characteristics are simplicity, neatness, and quiet. On the first floor the quiet couple have their pleasant parlor, and their snug little sitting room, with kitchen adjoining, and they have two good chambers above. The curved form of the roof, while it makes the attic more commodious, has a substantial and pleasing look."

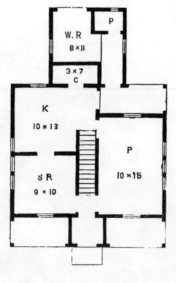

FIRST-FLOOR PLAN.

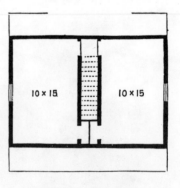

SECOND-FLOOR PLAN.

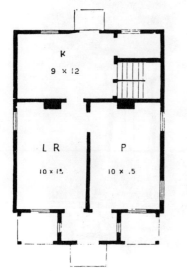

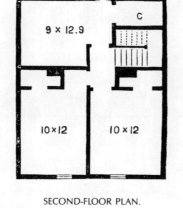

FIRST-FLOOR PLAN.

SECOND-FLOOR PLAN.

A second modest design from Cleaveland, Backus, and Backus also cost less than $1,000. It allowed for a front hall, a parlor, and a sitting or living room—each with fireplaces—and an elaborate verandah. The front windows reach to the floor and open like the entrance door, "for the better enjoyment of the verandah."

Old buildings were recycled for new uses in the nineteeth century just as they are today. The design shown here was originally a one-story coach house 20' square. Five feet were added to the depth, creating space for a stairway to a second floor, a front hall, and a pantry (off the living room). The living room also served as the kitchen and dining room. The steeply pitched roof allows for three large bedrooms. This redesigned building was included in *Village and Farm Cottages* by Cleaveland, Backus, and Backus. The renovation was said to have cost $900 in 1856.

L. R

P

10 × 15

10 × 15

FIRST-FLOOR PLAN.

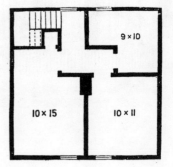

9 × 10

10 × 15   10 × 11

SECOND-FLOOR PLAN.

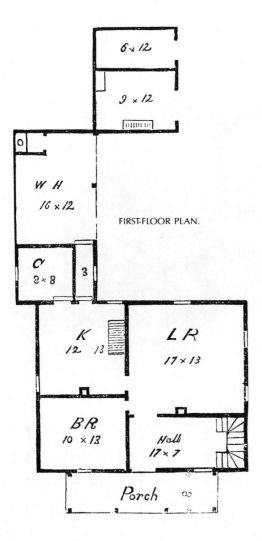

6 x 12

9 x 12

W H
16 x 12

FIRST-FLOOR PLAN.

C
9 x 8

3

K
12 x 13

L R
17 x 13

B R
10 x 13

Hall
17 x 7

Porch

Lewis Allen's Gothic Revival cottage is similar to many built across America in the mid-1800s. What sets it apart from the average example of the style are the side gables, which help to light the second-story bedrooms, and the boldly projecting eaves. Only a first-floor plan was given in *Rural Architecture* (1851). As shown, the building is essentially a square with a pantry ("C") and back hall tacked on one corner. The hall leads to a partially open wood house and a carriage house.

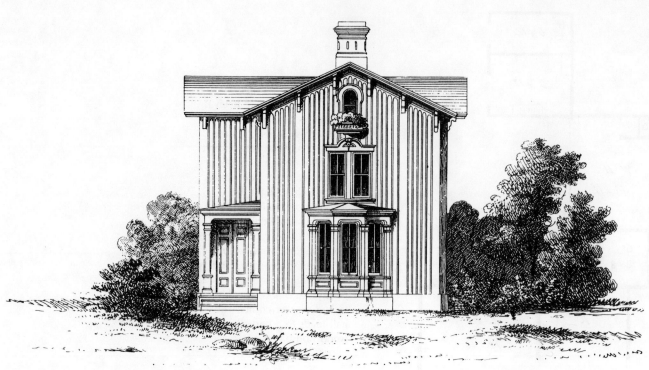

Cottages were not designed solely for small farmers or village workmen. By the 1850s numerous house plan books contained designs which would suit the prosperous businessman or the successful farmer. Samuel Sloan in *The Model Architect* (1852), volume 1, presented several plans for stylish cottages. What most of these plans have in common with the modest cottage is the use of board-and-batten siding, picturesque ornamentation, an irregular form, and moderately-sized rooms. This first Sloan design (others are illustrated on pages 34 and 35) is for a three-story cottage. It includes such amenities as a library, a bath, and a total of nine bedrooms. The parlor and sitting room are designated "drawing rooms," a stylistic pretension of the time. For a large family—with or without household help—this cottage would have been ideal.

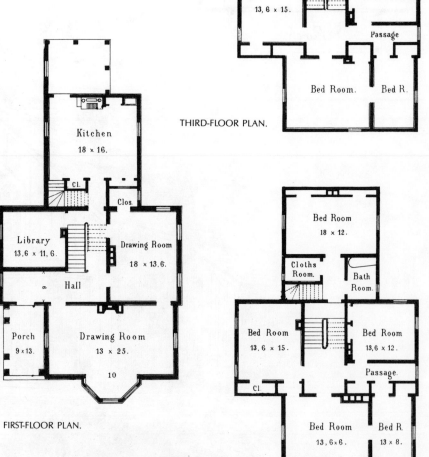

THIRD-FLOOR PLAN.

Bed Room
13, 6 × 15.

Bed Room

Passage

Bed Room.

Bed R.

FIRST-FLOOR PLAN.

Kitchen
18 × 16.

Cl.

Clos.

Library
13,6 × 11, 6.

Drawing Room
18 × 13,6.

Hall

Porch
9 × 13.

Drawing Room
13 × 25.

10

Bed Room
18 × 12.

Cloths Room.

Bath Room.

Bed Room
13, 6 × 15.

Bed Room
13,6 × 12.

Passage.

Cl.

Bed Room
13, 6 × 6.

Bed R.
13 × 8.

SECOND-FLOOR PLAN.

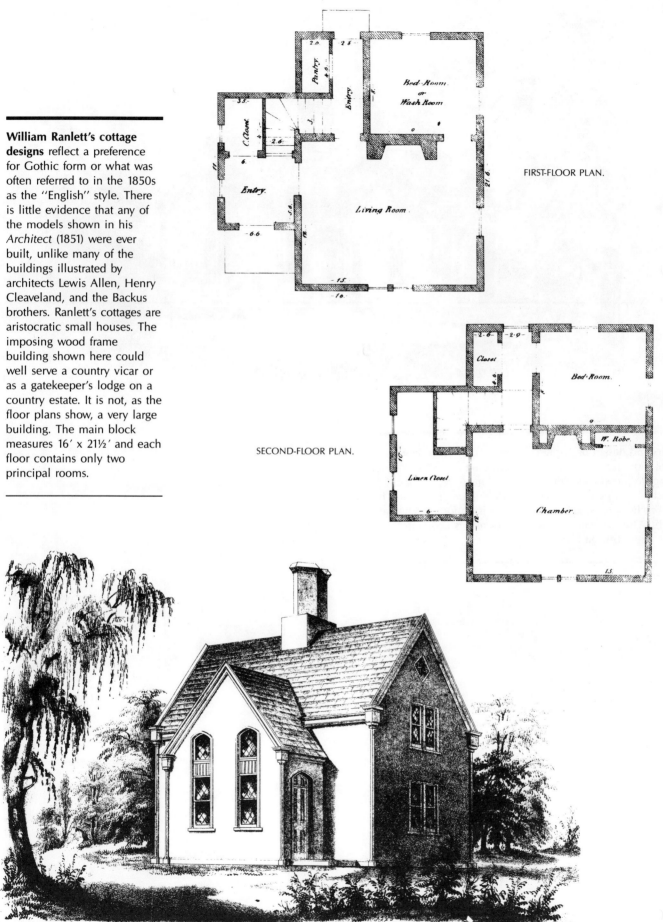

FIRST-FLOOR PLAN.

SECOND-FLOOR PLAN.

William Ranlett's cottage designs reflect a preference for Gothic form or what was often referred to in the 1850s as the ''English'' style. There is little evidence that any of the models shown in his *Architect* (1851) were ever built, unlike many of the buildings illustrated by architects Lewis Allen, Henry Cleaveland, and the Backus brothers. Ranlett's cottages are aristocratic small houses. The imposing wood frame building shown here could well serve a country vicar or as a gatekeeper's lodge on a country estate. It is not, as the floor plans show, a very large building. The main block measures 16′ x 21½′ and each floor contains only two principal rooms.

32

A second design by Ranlett is a bit more practical. In an attempt to present something ''rustic'' and homey, however, he has literally gone out on a limb. Whole timbers are used as corner posts and branches serve as cornice brackets. The building is clapboard-sided and measures 20' x 28', excluding the front hall. There is provision for a kitchen and a downstairs bedroom.

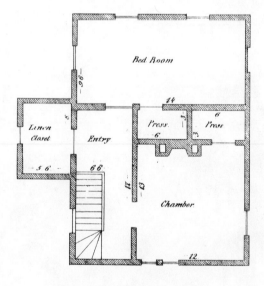

SECOND-FLOOR PLAN.

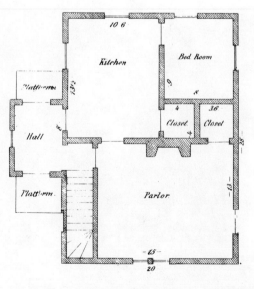

FIRST-FLOOR PLAN.

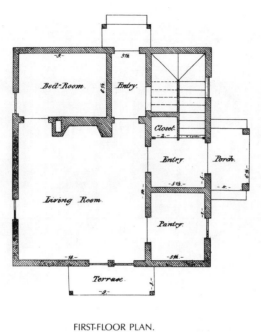

FIRST-FLOOR PLAN.

SECOND-FLOOR PLAN.

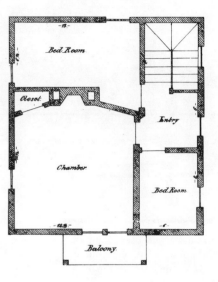

A classic "English" style cottage of wood-frame construction is a third Ranlett design. The decorative gable vergeboards, balconies, terraces, and arched porch endow the building with a romantic character. This was a home, Ranlett wrote, "for the better class of laborers and mechanics." As in the first cottage plan (p. 31), cooking was to be done in the living room.

34

Samuel Sloan used many of
the conventions of Gothic cottage architecture in this two-
story dwelling illustrated in
the second volume of *The
Model Architect* (1852).
"There are thousands of working men in this country," he
wrote, "who wish to give
something of beauty and
interest to the simple forms of
cottage life." Board-and-batten
siding sets the overall stylistic
character of this house. The
highly decorative roof with
finials and cresting is frosting
on the cake. Enormous
brackets support the wide roof
overhang. The windows also
reflect the Gothic style, those
in the upper story being composed of diamond panes, and
the lower windows, a com-
bination of diamond and
square. Adding further to the
gingerbread appearance is the
handsome fretwork-paneled
porch.

The floor plans are for a con-
ventional two-story center-hall
cottage measuring approx-
imately 20½′ x 34′.

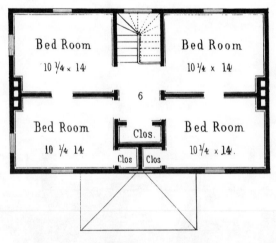

SECOND-FLOOR PLAN.

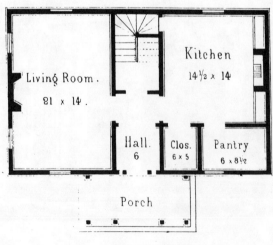

FIRST-FLOOR PLAN.

A second Sloan design is entitled a "Cheap Cottage" in *The Model Architect*, volume 2. It is a two-family or double house split exactly down the middle into two units. The first floor contains matching living rooms and kitchens. Each unit has its own front and side entrances. No plan was provided for the second floor, but Sloan intended each unit to have two bedrooms. The overall cost was estimated at $1,800, or $900 each.

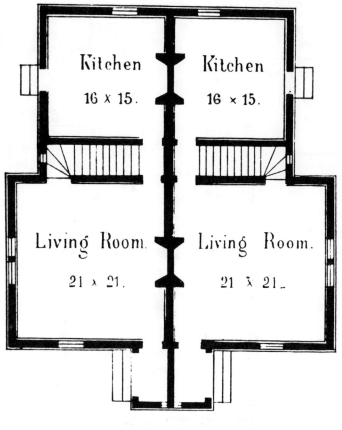

FIRST-FLOOR PLAN.

36

The irregularity of form
favored by fashionable architects in the 1850s gradually
won popular acceptance.
Added to Andrew Jackson
Downing's classic *Cottage
Residences*, first published in
the 1840s, in a new edition
dating from 1873, is this
design for a ''Side-Hill Cottage.'' Its author is George E.
Harney, editor of the revised
volume, and its style reflects
the coming vogue for the
''Elizabethan'' or English
Tudor cottage. The cost,
$3,200, was high, but building
costs, as Harney notes in his
introduction, had escalated
greatly since the Civil War.
Since the cottage is built into
the side of a hill, good use is
made of a partially exposed
cellar. The kitchen is located
here as well as a bedroom.
For ventilation, both rooms
are positioned in the most
open area. Since the dining
room is situated on the main
floor, a dumbwaiter is provided to carry food upstairs from
the kitchen. One small and
two large bedrooms are
enclosed under the steeply
overhanging roof composed of
polychromed shingles. The
cellar walls are of stone, but
the rest of the building is of
frame construction.

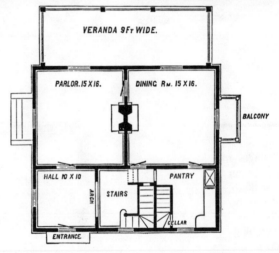

MAIN FLOOR PLAN.

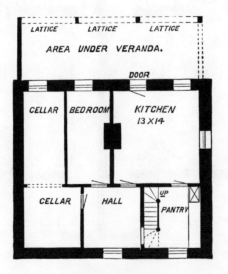

BASEMENT FLOOR PLAN.

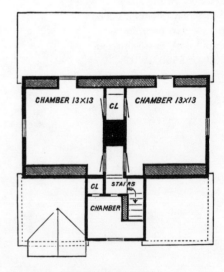

SECOND-FLOOR PLAN.

2.

HOMES FOR THE WORKINGMAN'S FAMILY:

The Mid-Victorian Cottage

By the 1850s and '60s plans for simple cottages were commonly available and widely copied from books and periodicals. The designs ranged from 3- or 4-room one-story houses suitable for a workingman's family to more ambitious and ornamental two-story dwellings with as many as six rooms. These larger cottages were intended primarily for the lower-middle-class family. All the houses were built with a basement or cellar which might house the kitchen as well as a laundry and storage area for foodstuffs. Central heating had been introduced by this time, but it was not a convenience within reach of the average homeowner. In their cottages, stoves took the place of a furnace, and in some a fireplace was still used for heat. With indoor plumbing a luxury for the few, bathrooms, of course, were nonexistent in all but the most expensive cottages.

Daniel T. Atwood, A. J. Bicknell, and the New York architectural firm of Palliser, Palliser & Co. were among the popular published contributors of house plan designs during this period. The influence of the Downing school can still be seen in the ornamentation of their buildings, but the style gradually changed from the Gothic to the Italianate, Mansard, and Queen Anne. With these shifts in style also came changes in form as buildings assumed asymmetric rather than symmetric shapes. Verandahs wrapped around two sides of a house and the main entrance came to be located to one side of a house rather than at its center. Porches were often recessed instead of projecting from the building.

These changes were to some extent a reflection of better economic times. The average wage earner after the Civil War could afford a larger house, the addition of a wing, a second story, even a dining room. In his design for a suburban cottage illustrated on the opposite page, George E. Woodward provided for a future addition that would double the size of his modest cottage. Other architects emphasized the benefits of an entry hall or vestibule and even ventured to suggest a bathroom. If at all possible, the kitchen was placed on the more convenient first floor rather than in the basement.

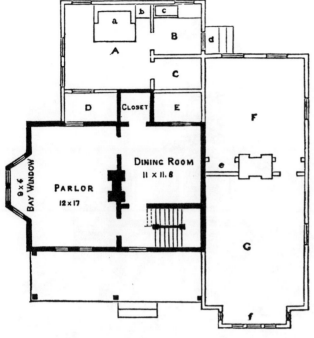

FIRST-FLOOR PLAN.

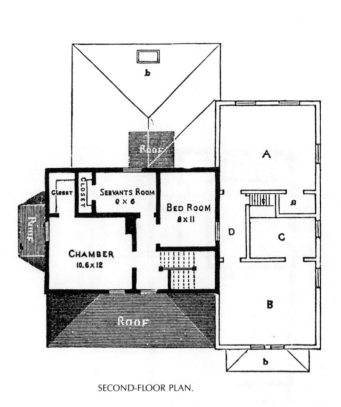

SECOND-FLOOR PLAN.

George E. Woodward in *Woodward's Architecture and Rural Art* (1867), presented a plan for a suburban cottage which could be enlarged at a later date. He recommended starting small: "Let one live in ever so humble a cottage . . . . If furnished and embellished in good taste, it rather advances the [social] position than otherwise." Woodward called his plan one of "moderate pretensions" and estimated that it could be built in the New York City area for $1,500 to $1,800, but refused to speculate on the cost of future additions. The floor plans show the original layout (dark lines) and additions (light open lines). The kitchen and laundry room are originally included in the basement; provision is made for their future placement on ground level (spaces marked "A" and "B" on the first-floor plan).

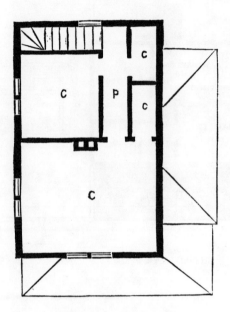

SECOND-FLOOR PLAN.

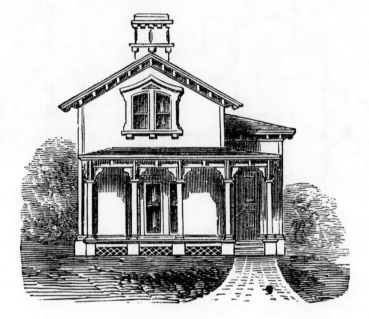

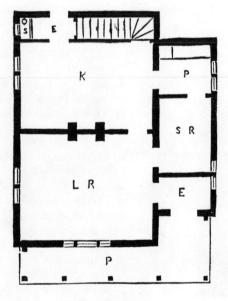

FIRST-FLOOR PLAN.

Daniel T. Atwood included a number of handsome cottage designs in *Atwood's Country and Suburban Houses* (1871), published by Orange Judd & Co. Judd was also the publisher of the influential *American Agriculturist*, and it was in this monthly publication that some of Atwood's plans first appeared in the 1860s and '70s. This design is termed "A Mechanic's Cottage" and was expected to cost $1,400. One unusual but practical feature of the house is the placement of the stairway at the rear, off the kitchen in the manner of a simple Colonial home. Other features are completely "modern" for the time, including the wraparound verandah, bay window, ornamental window framing, and bracketed cornice. The house is wood-framed and presumably sided with clapboards.

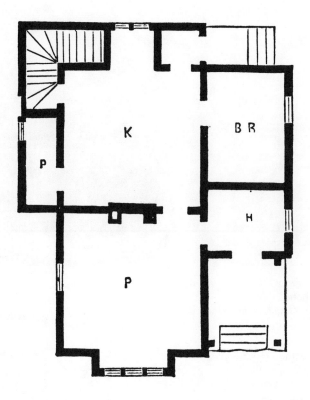

FIRST-FLOOR PLAN.

Atwood supplied a second design for his model work-ingman's cottage. It varies only slightly in outline from the first, there being a side entry porch rather than a full verandah. The floor plan is a bit more irregular, and the stairs are compressed to form tightwinders. The cost, $1,400, is the same. The second floor, a plan for which is not shown, contains three bed-rooms rather than two.

Decidedly neo-classical in style is the symmetrical cottage designed by Daniel T. Atwood. It could be used as a gate lodge or as a separate "tasteful home for the clerk or mechanic just starting in life." The cost: $2,000. The overall size is 16' x 26'. The verandah, or as Atwood termed it, the "piazza," is 6½' wide and wraps completely around the front of the house. In style, the plan is decidedly old-fashioned for its time. Among its most handsome features are the round-headed tripartite windows on the first and second floors. Together with the piazza and wide roof overhang, these features suggest a small Italian villa.

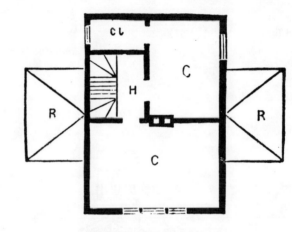

SECOND-FLOOR PLAN.

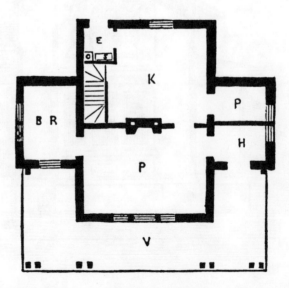

FIRST-FLOOR PLAN.

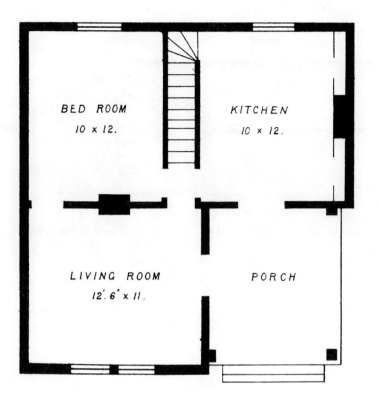

BED ROOM
10 x 12.

KITCHEN
10 x 12.

LIVING ROOM
12'. 6" x 11.

PORCH

FIRST-FLOOR PLAN.

Termed a "cheap frame cottage," this house from A. J. Bicknell's *Village Builder* (1872) makes the most practical use of very limited space. There is no front entry hall, and stairs to the second floor ascend from a corner of the kitchen. Significantly, the architect has not designated the front room a parlor but a living room, this not being a house of any pretended elegance. A second-floor plan has not been provided. While the master bedroom is located on the first floor, as many as three very small bedrooms might be tucked under the eaves of the hip roof. The cost of the building was estimated at $750.

A second "cheap" design presented by A. J. Bicknell is more ambitious in scope and would cost almost twice as much as the frame cottage illustrated on page 43. There is a center stair hall which opens off the corner entry porch and leads to the kitchen, dining room, and parlor. The rooms are larger in this model than in the former, there being more than 100 square feet additional living space on each floor.

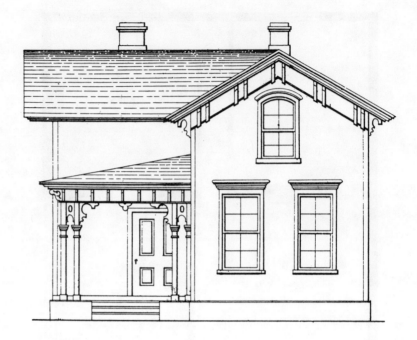

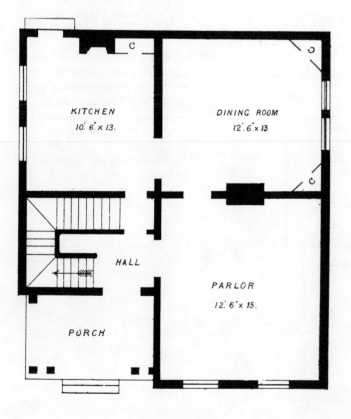

FIRST-FLOOR PLAN.

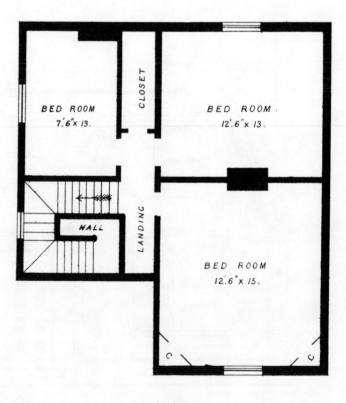

SECOND-FLOOR PLAN.

SECOND-FLOOR PLAN.

CHAMBER.
13.6 × 15.

BATH ROOM.

CHAMBER.
14 × 14.

CHAMBER.
11.6 × 15.

BED ROOM
6 × 11.

FIRST-FLOOR PLAN.

PANTRY

SINK

ENTRY

SITTING ROOM.
13.6 × 17.

TO CELLAR

KITCHEN
14 × 14

HALL.

UP

PARLOR.
15 × 18.

PIAZZA.

PORCH

Lyman Underwood of Boston was the architect of what Bicknell referred to as a "French" cottage because of its mansard roof. It is an elegant design distinguished by very fine framing and trim. The roof is made of slate, while the side porch, termed a "piazza," and the side bay are roofed with tin. The interior finish is similarly choice, with ample provision for storage areas and convenient inside plumbing. Three chimneys carry flues for stoves and fireplaces. The walls are clapboarded with Eastern pine. This 1872 cottage, intended for a small family without household help, cost approximately $3,800 to erect and finish.

Increasingly popular by the 1880s were houses designed in what has been termed the Shingle style because of the use of cut shingles for covering exterior walls. Shingles could be used effectively to decorate even the simplest cottage included in Palliser, Palliser & Co.'s *New Cottage Homes and Details* (1887), of which this plan is a typical example. One of the building's chief virtues is its low cost—$450. In addition to the shingling, there are other small amenities which recommend this modest plan—an entry porch with a half-moon design, a small entry hall, and a good supply of storage closets. The kitchen must have been located in the cellar, a decided limitation.

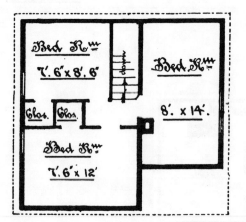

SECOND-FLOOR PLAN.

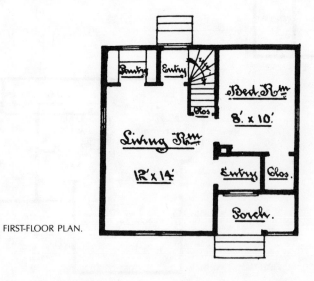

FIRST-FLOOR PLAN.

A second small cottage from
the Palliser collection is close
to the Queen Anne style and
makes limited use of
shingling. In plan it is very
straightforward, being a tall
two-story rectangle with a
shed extension at one side.
Space for cooking is provided
on the first floor rather than
in the basement. The first
floor is 8′ high and the
second, 7½′. The bedrooms
are small, but their relatively
high ceilings make them
appear more spacious. Considerable gingerbread
decorates the roof line, a
feature also incorporated in
the front and back porches.
The original cost was no more
than $400.

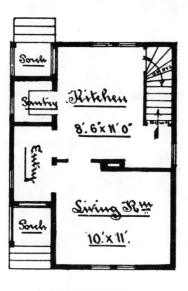

FIRST-FLOOR PLAN.

SECOND-FLOOR PLAN.

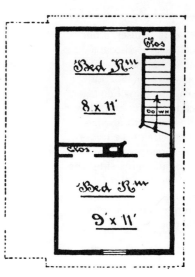

According to Palliser, a one-story cottage, ''well-adapted to the wants of a small family,'' could be built in 1887 for $550. Palliser's small cottage is an early form of bungalow, with the bedrooms arranged along one side of the house and the living room and kitchen on the other side. The design is pleasant and features a handsome bay window and an entry protected by a hood and stoop.

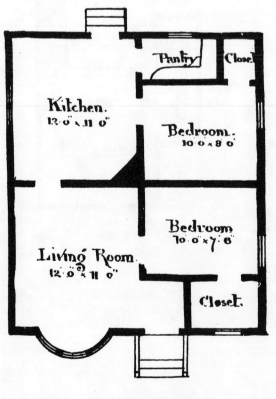

Pantry   Closet

Kitchen.
12·0 x 11·0

Bedroom.
10·0 x 8·0

Bedroom
10·0 x 7·6

Living Room
12·0 x 11·0

Closet.

GROUND-FLOOR PLAN.

FRONT ELEVATION.

SIDE ELEVATION.

REAR ELEVATION.

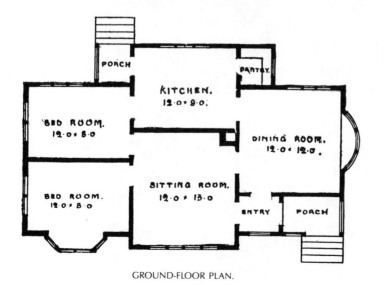

GROUND-FLOOR PLAN.

PORCH

KITCHEN.
12·0×9·0.

PANTRY.

BED ROOM.
12·0×8·0

DINING ROOM.
12·0×12·0.

BED ROOM.
12·0×8·0

SITTING ROOM.
12·0×13·0

ENTRY

PORCH

The Palliser design shown here might be better termed a lodge than a cottage. The long one-and-a-half story building was suggested as an estate house for a gardener or coachman. As the three elevations show, the building is handsomely appointed with shingles, clapboards, large windows, and ornate trim. There are only five rooms, but, because of the irregularity of the plan, one room does not simply flow into another. The space has many interesting angles.

What Daniel T. Atwood called a "half-timbered cottage" in his *Country and Suburban Houses* (1871) was designed, like the plan on the preceding page, as a lodge or gatehouse. With roof cresting, decorative gable bargeboards, finials, and bracketed gables and dormers, it is highly picturesque. The first-floor walls are horizontally boarded; those of the second floor are vertically positioned. The form of the house is of two rectangles set at right angles to each other. Principal rooms on each floor are in the front part of the house, with service rooms in the rear. The second floor rear includes both a bathroom and a servant's room.

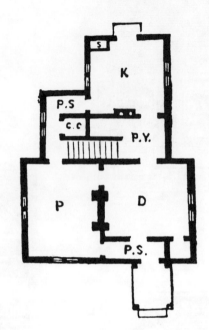

FIRST-FLOOR PLAN.

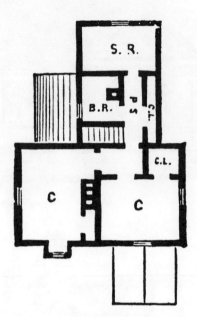

SECOND-FLOOR PLAN.

FRONT ELEVATION.

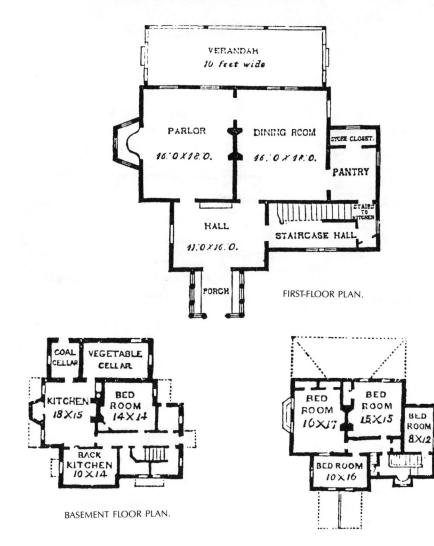

FIRST-FLOOR PLAN.

VERANDAH
10 feet wide

PARLOR
16.'0 X 18.'0.

DINING ROOM
16.'0 X 18.'0.

STORE CLOSET.

PANTRY

STAIRS TO KITCHEN

HALL
11.'0 X 16.'0.

STAIRCASE HALL

PORCH

BASEMENT FLOOR PLAN.

COAL CELLAR

VEGETABLE CELLAR

KITCHEN
18 X 15

BED ROOM
14 X 14

BACK KITCHEN
10 X 14

SECOND-FLOOR PLAN.

BED ROOM
16 X 17

BED ROOM
15 X 15

BED ROOM
8 X 12

BED ROOM
10 X 16

Calvert Vaux did not design cottages for the workingman, but for gentlemen of some leisure. His design for a rural cottage, published in *Villas and Cottages* (1864), was built by a Dr. de la Montagnie of Fishkill Landing, New York. Because the house is positioned on a slope, special advantage is taken of the lower or basement level. Both a kitchen and a bedroom are found here, in addition to the usual storage rooms. The elevation shows the sprawling low profile of the cottage, a form emphasized by the clipped gables at each end of the building and the wide roof overhang. Vaux claimed that the cottage would cost about $2,900, this because "by wooden construction . . . picturesque breaks in the plan may be made for less money than they will cost in brickwork . . . . It requires considerable time and care to make a brick corner plumb and true, while a wooden angle can be easily worked."

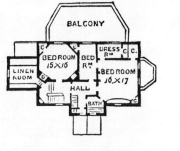

SECOND-FLOOR PLAN.

ATTIC FLOOR PLAN.

FIRST-FLOOR PLAN.

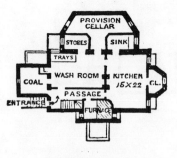

BASEMENT FLOOR PLAN.

It is difficult to believe that Calvert Vaux considered this imposing building a "model cottage," but that is what he termed it. Today, it would be considered a small mansion. Vaux found it perfect for a small family and boasted that his "design has been . . . arranged for the use of a man of simple habits, with some refinement of taste." The cost of building this house of wood in 1864 was estimated at $3,500. With a center pavillion and hip roof, the building most resembles a Georgian Colonial mansion in form. To this Vaux has added a romantic entrance porch, balconies, window bays, a broad verandah, and ornamental window caps and gable trim. Inside, there is ample space for a family of three or four children, there being three bedrooms on the second floor and two or three more in the attic. All the bedrooms are provided with closets, the master bedroom on the second floor also including a dressing room and connecting bath.

A cottage in the Italianate style, one of the several popular revival styles of the mid- to late 19th century, was designed by E. R. Francisco of Kansas City and published in A. J. Bicknell's *Village Builder* (1872). The design is distinguished by the wide roof overhang, the drop pendants affixed to each corner of the cornice, and the several balconies. The main section of the frame building measures approximately 33½′ x 15′, and attached to this is a rear kitchen and a two-story side entry and stair hall. The building cost was $2,000, a modest sum for the time.

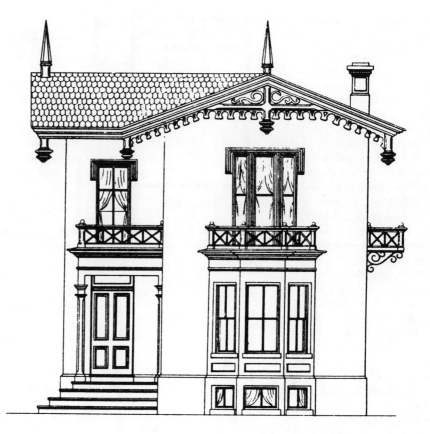

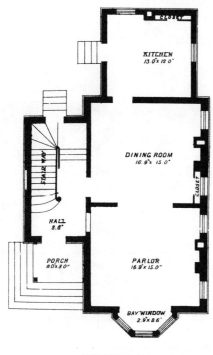

FIRST-FLOOR PLAN.

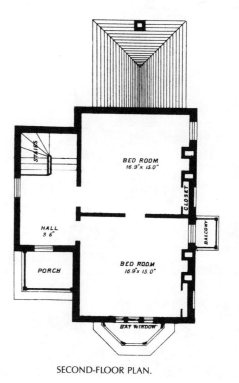

SECOND-FLOOR PLAN.

This Queen Anne-style cottage suitable for a small suburban lot was featured in *Palliser's New Cottage Homes and Details* (1887). Planned to cost only $2,475, the house was recommended as "excellently suited to the wants of the thrifty and sensible mechanic whose wife will not be above the point where she is willing to contribute her help by a proper and economical care of her own household wants and duties." In other words, there was to be no household help. The kitchen is unusually spacious, measuring 13′ x 15′ so that there would be "ample room for all domestic living purposes." Four principal bedrooms are well laid out on the second floor, and a fifth room, designated a bedroom, could be changed, the architects suggested, to a bathroom. What this additional cost would be was not provided.

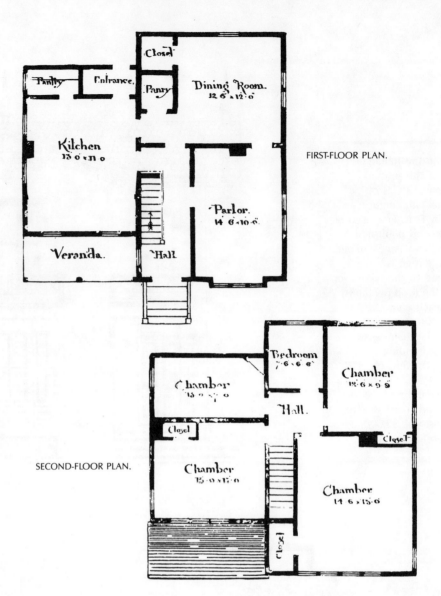

FIRST-FLOOR PLAN.

SECOND-FLOOR PLAN.

FRONT ELEVATION.

SIDE ELEVATION.

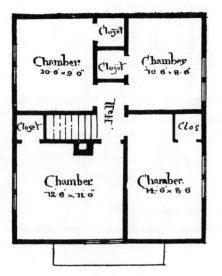

SECOND-FLOOR PLAN.

FRONT ELEVATION.

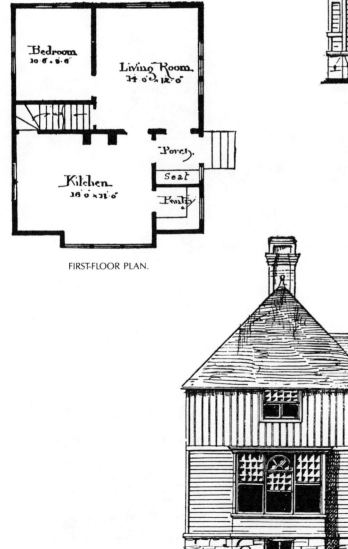

FIRST-FLOOR PLAN.

SIDE ELEVATION.

This square Queen Anne cottage plan, published by Palliser, Palliser & Co., is very simple and was designed to give "the greatest amount of room for the least possible outlay." Large enough for a family with three or four children, the house cost an estimated $1,375 in 1887. Considerable architectural distinction is achieved by using board-and-batten siding on the second floor and clapboards on the first. The recessed porch entryway, with seat, is another picturesque feature which does not add to the basic cost of the building. The architects, however, have not included a bathroom, an amenity that was becoming more and more common in the 1880s in even a modest cottage.

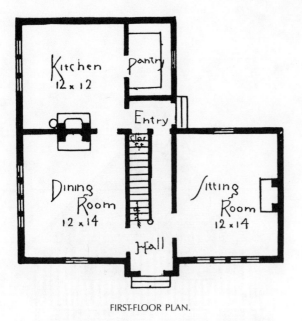

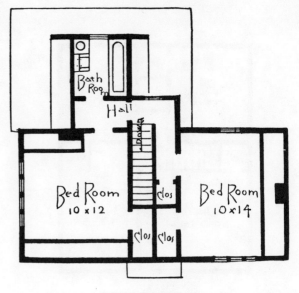

FIRST-FLOOR PLAN.

SECOND-FLOOR PLAN.

FRONT ELEVATION.

Among the most handsome and least expensive of Palliser cottage designs is this house constructed of brick on the first floor and of wood—with shingling—above. The architects claimed that its cost in 1887 was only from $1,200 to $1,400. It is not a large building, containing as it does less than 800 square feet of living space, but maximum use has been made of the space. Note especially how a bathroom has been tucked in under the eaves above the kitchen.

SIDE ELEVATION.

3.

PLACES OF REST AND RELAXATION:
The Late Victorian Cottage

The average cottage grew larger in size and more decorative in detail as the 19th century progressed. Despite this trend, the cottage continued to be viewed popularly as an informal exercise in the art of building, as a place of lesser social significance than the middle-class residence or villa of the rich. In part, the continuation of this prosaic image during the last decades of the 1800s was a result of economic good fortune. More and more people were able to build cottages as second homes, places to which they could retreat for relaxation during the summer months. In this regard, they were very much like their democratic presidents Grant and Garfield who resided in an executive mansion most of the year and moved to a cottage on the Jersey shore each summer. Many thousands of American families resided in summer cottages at the seaside, along the lake shore, or in the mountains. Those who could not afford to build or rent such picturesque retreats sought boarding houses or another inexpensive alternative, the cabin.

Vacation cottages remain among the most attractive and delightful features of the late-Victorian landscape. They are often laden with wooden ornamentation, gingerbread cut by jig saw and easily applied. Other cottages appear encased in shingles, their varied shapes forming interesting patterns. Nearly every vacation cottage is blessed with a wide porch or verandah and a balcony or two from which to enjoy fair weather.

Many summer cottages were very cheaply built. Few required a basement and none needed a furnace. A bathroom was often not included, a privy considered adequate for the needs of vacationers. Storage space was not an important consideration, and closets were consequently small.

Illustrated here and on the following two pages are designs for six seaside vacation cottages in the Queen Anne style. These were first presented in *Modern Architectural Designs and Details* (1881) by William T. Comstock, a New York architect. None of the designs include floor plans. Each of the wood frame buildings is marked by the use of clapboards and ornate gable trim. In at least five of the designs there are elaborate gingerbread porches, verandahs, and balconies—all convenient fair-weather observation posts.

Each cottage is raised several feet aboveground, a practical step in any area barely above sea level and prone to seasonal flooding. Note the use of louvered window and door shutters in the designs shown on the next page. There was often a need in coastal areas to protect a cottage from battering winds.

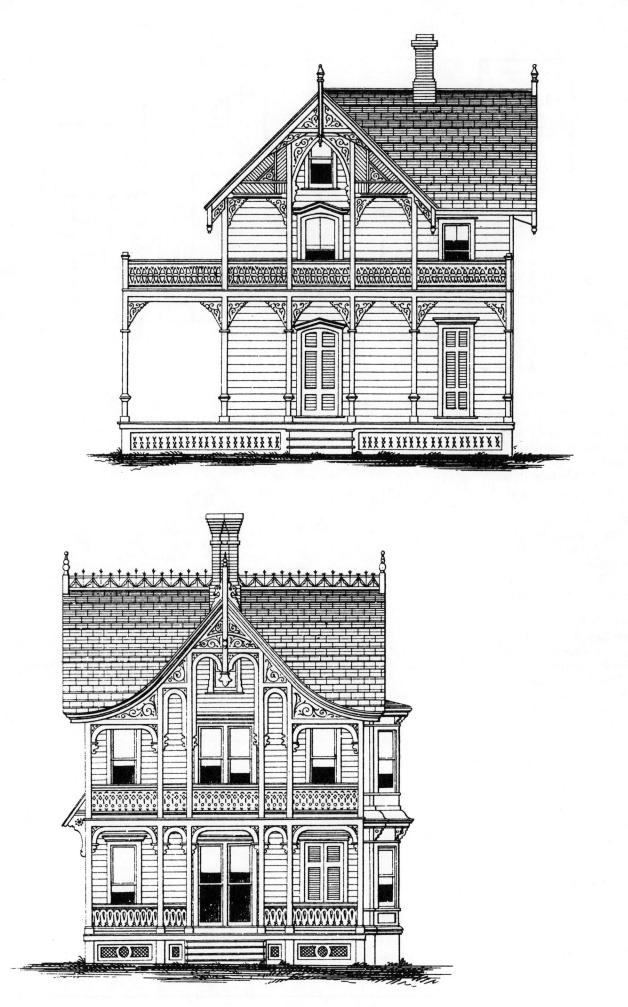

FIRST-FLOOR PLAN.

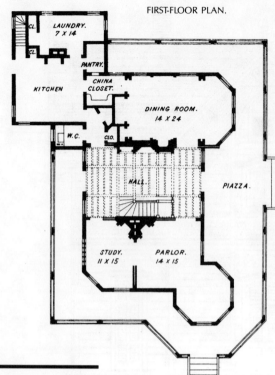

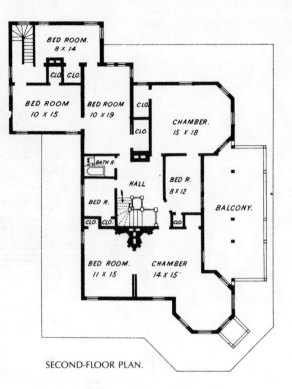

SECOND-FLOOR PLAN.

J. Pickering Putnam's "Lake View Cottage" plans were featured in Comstock's *Modern Architectural Designs and Details.* An extremely ambitious design, it is not unlike some of the impressive seashore cottages built in New England at the time. Putnam, a Boston architect, spared few domestic touches in this raised and shingled cottage. A summer home it was to be, but yet a summer home offering many of the same amenities of a city or suburban residence. A verandah wraps around seven-eighths of the structure and included are several additional balconies from which one could enjoy the outdoors. The center first-floor hall is immense and was perhaps so scaled to allow for maximum cross ventilation. This wide hall neatly divides the kitchen and dining room from the study and parlor. There is a total of eleven bedrooms, three of which are included on the attic floor and were probably intended for servants. Baths are on both the first and second floors.

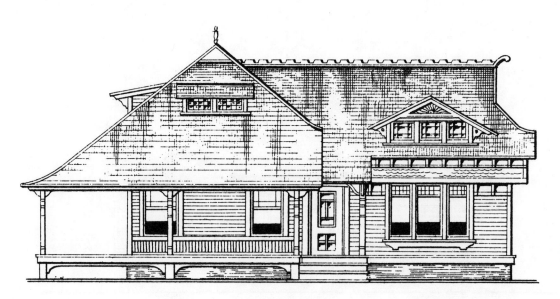

FRONT ELEVATION.

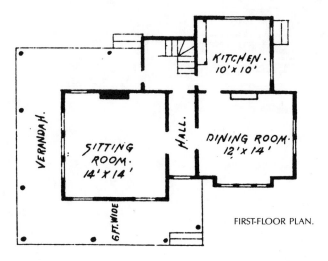

KITCHEN.
10'×10'

VERANDAH.

SITTING
ROOM.
14'×14'

HALL.

DINING ROOM.
12'×14'

6 FT. WIDE

FIRST-FLOOR PLAN.

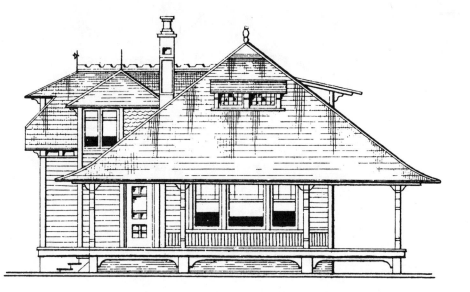

SIDE ELEVATION.

William B. Tuthill, architect of Carnegie Hall in New York, contributed three "Small Seashore or Southern Cottage" designs to Comstock's *Modern Architectural Designs and Details*. These are shown here and on the succeeding two pages. What is exceptional about the first cottage on this page and the third on page 65 is their modernity. The strong horizontal lines, sweeping low roofs, and framing members resemble those found in later Western houses by brothers Charles Sumner Greene and Henry Mather Greene and in the work of Bernard Maybeck. Both cottages suggest the style of the early Prairie School of Frank Lloyd Wright. The second design on the next page is more formally Queen Anne, there being a massing of tower, steeply pitched roofs, and wraparound verandah.

The floor plan of each cottage is relatively simple, the first floor consisting of an entry hall, sitting room, kitchen, and dining room. Second-floor plans were not provided by Tuthill.

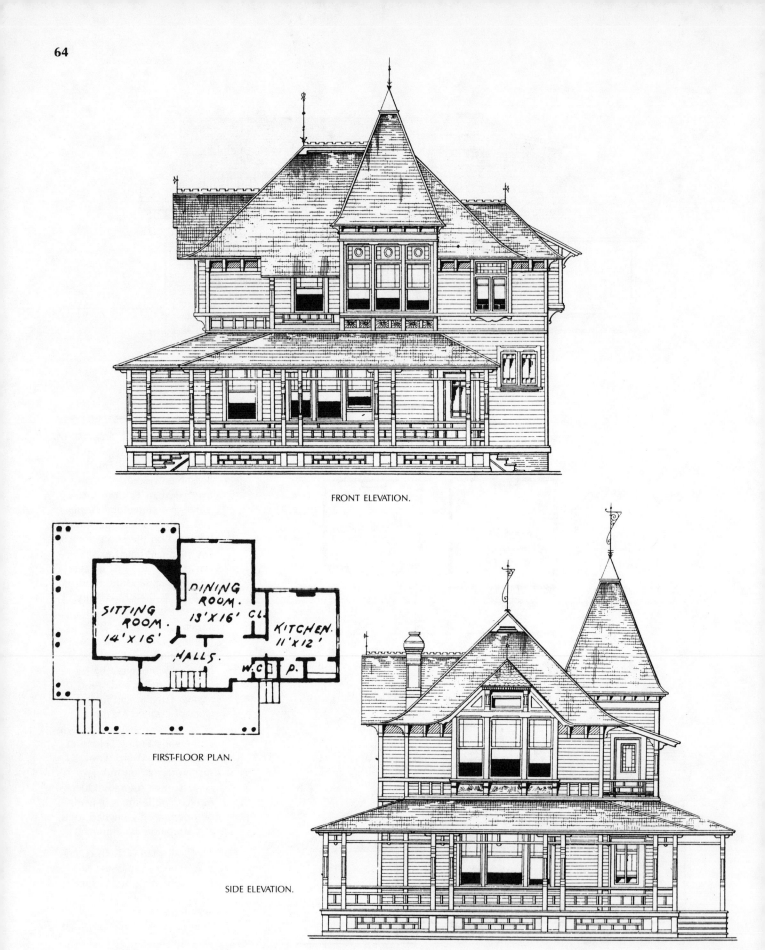

FRONT ELEVATION.

SITTING ROOM. 14'X16'

DINING ROOM. 13'X16'

CL.

KITCHEN. 11'X12'

HALLS.

W.C. P.

FIRST-FLOOR PLAN.

SIDE ELEVATION.

FRONT ELEVATION:

FIRST-FLOOR PLAN.

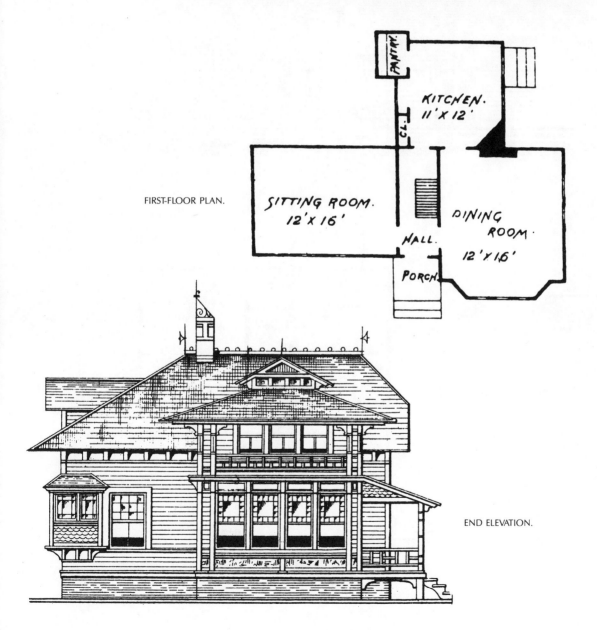

PANTRY

KITCHEN.
11' X 12'

CL.

SITTING ROOM.
12' X 16'

DINING
ROOM.
12' X 16'

HALL.

PORCH.

END ELEVATION.

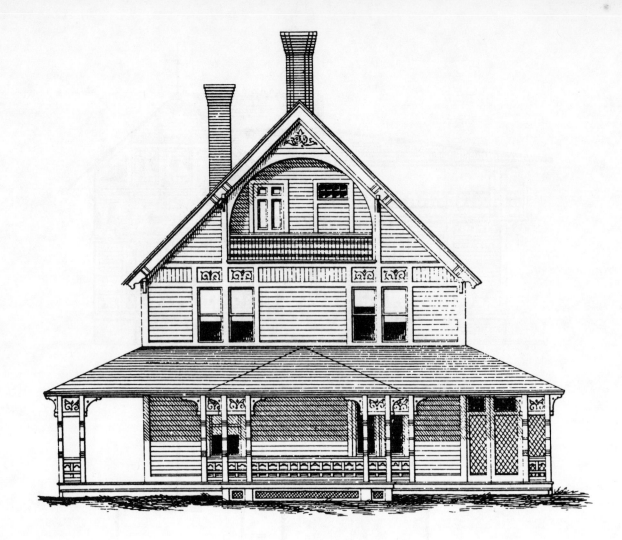

William T. Comstock himself might have been the architect of this vacation cottage, one of the many unattributed designs in his *Modern Architectural Designs and Details* (1881). It is simply a two-story rectangle with a wraparound verandah and a cut-away third-story balcony. An unusual feature is the "dining piazza," partially enclosed by the second story. Four bedrooms were located on the second floor.

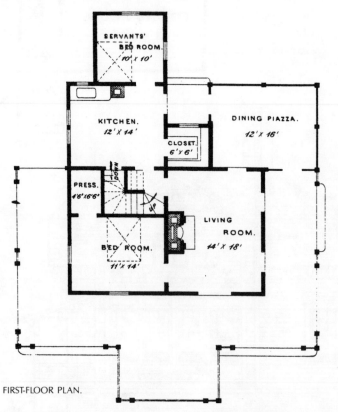

SERVANTS'
BED ROOM.
10' X 10'

KITCHEN.
12' X 14'

DINING PIAZZA.
12' X 16'

CLOSET.
6' X 6'

PRESS.
4'6"X6'6"

DOWN

UP

LIVING
ROOM.
14' X 18'

BED ROOM.
11' X 14'

FIRST-FLOOR PLAN.

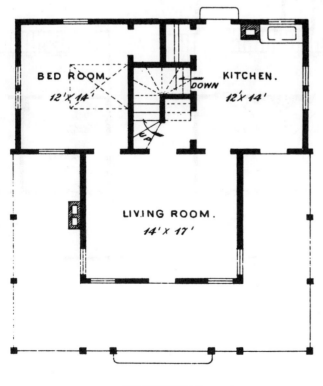

FIRST-FLOOR PLAN.

A second design attributed to Comstock is more compact and horizontal in form than that on the opposite page. The three-sided verandah provides ventilation for the three first-floor rooms, and cut away from the broad overhanging roof is a pleasant balcony. Three bedrooms are included on the second floor.

FRONT ELEVATION.

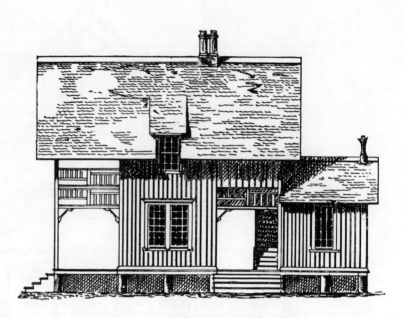

SIDE ELEVATION.

The architectural firm of Palliser, Palliser & Co. of New York intended some of its vacation cottage designs for semitropical regions. Palm trees were included in the renderings so that there would be no doubt as to the buildings' regional character. Illustrated on this page and the following page are two cottages which would have been suitable for the Florida coast or the Texas Gulf coast. Each design is a rather delicate composition of framing in the Stick style. And in each case, a simple layout of rooms is enclosed on almost all sides by porches or a verandah enclosed on the first-floor level. On the second floor, bedrooms open to balconies which fill the space between the overhanging upper gable roof and the lower verandah roof. The drawings are from the architectural firm's *New Cottage Homes and Details* (1887).

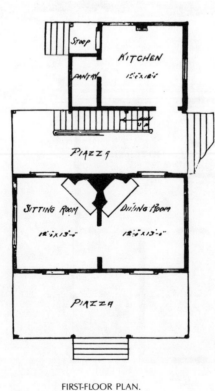

FIRST-FLOOR PLAN.

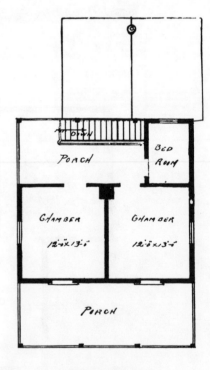

SECOND-FLOOR PLAN.

FRONT ELEVATION.

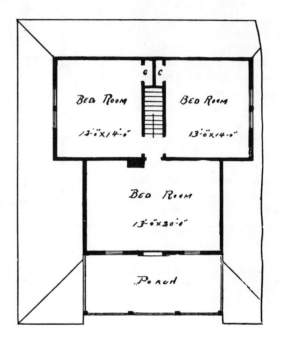

SECOND-FLOOR PLAN.

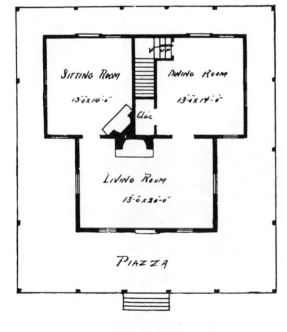

FIRST-FLOOR PLAN.

SIDE ELEVATION.

Most summer cottages, however grandiose, were of frame construction. This lakeside cottage designed by Gould & Angell, architects, of Providence, R.I., was built of red brick with wood frame upper stories. It is a four-square building, essentially Romanesque in style, but partaking of Eastlake detailing and making heavy use of shingling. The cottage is, indeed, a country mansion with a total of eight bedrooms, one with its own dressing room. There is one bathroom on the second floor which must have been a busy place on a summer morning.

FIRST-FLOOR PLAN.

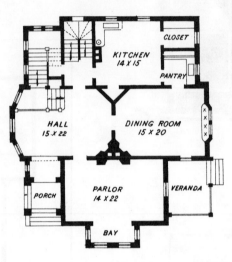

SECOND-FLOOR PLAN.

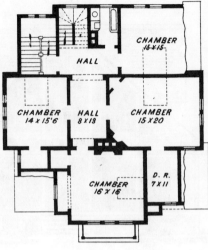

4.

MODERN TIMES:
The Spanish, English, and
Colonial Revival
Bungalow and Cottage

The demand for low-cost, one-family housing in the early 20th century led to an extraordinary expansion of urban and suburban areas. To be able to own a home, however humble, was the dream of millions of young couples. Because of the automobile and increasingly sophisticated transportation systems, whole new neighborhoods could be created on the outskirts of town, and large tracts of land beyond were opened to suburban real estate speculation. Unlike the situation which has prevailed since World War II, developers of land and builders rarely worked in tandem. Simply, the land was prepared for building. What you did with it was your own business. Many couples had no choice in the matter and became their own builders. And for plans they turned to books and magazines.

In the early 1900s there was a sharp departure from the late-Victorian fashion for angular, asymmetrical buildings in the Queen Anne style to houses with more regular and horizontal lines. The revival of the Colonial form was readily adopted and adapted by the designers of cottages. Some of the architects preferred to use either early New England cottages or timbered English farmhouses as their models; others turned to the Spanish Colonial or Mission-style building for inspiration. And there were the proponents of the bungalow—a low, narrow building with a sloping roof enclosing a front porch. The bungalow was an especially attractive alternative for one seeking an economical building plan. It could be built on a small, inexpensive lot and, because of its gradually sloping roof line, offered optimum living space. The classic bungalow of this period is a very compact self-contained structure with little or no expensive add-ons such as exterior porches or wings. By the 1920s, however, the term "bungalow" was being applied to almost every kind of small building and was used interchangeably with the term "cottage."

The buildings illustrated in the following pages reflect all of the design features of the period. Except for an introductory plan from *The Craftsman*, the plans have been chosen from two books, *Homes of Character* (1923) by a Boston architect, Robert L. Stevenson, and *Small Homes of Architectural Distinction* (1929) a compilation produced by The Architects' Small House Service Bureau of the American Institute of Architects and edited by Robert T. Jones. Both books address the concerns of the prospective homeowner who cannot afford the services of a professional architect but wishes to have a house planned, as Stevenson writes, "with an idea of comfort and convenience as well as artistic merit."

The cottages of the 20th century contain nearly all of the appointments considered modern today—indoor plumbing, central heating if located in a region requiring such a system, and a good-sized kitchen. The kitchen is not as streamlined or as equipped with gadgets as it would become later, but there is a suggestion in some plans of what was called a scientific approach to food preparation. Many of these cottages also include such features particular to the period as breakfast and dining nooks, bed closets, and fireplace nooks. These were space-saving amenities that also added considerable charm.

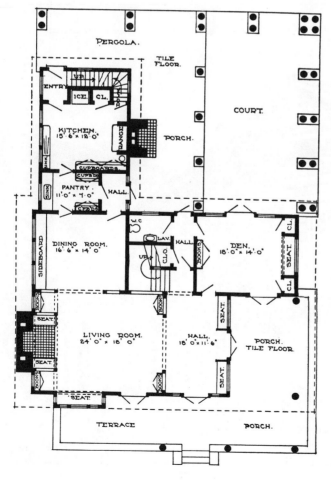

FIRST-FLOOR PLAN.

The Craftsman was one of the most influential home design magazines of the early 1900s. Its aesthetic of rustic utilitarianism, as championed by Gustave Stickley, found echoes in the contemporary Arts and Crafts movement, and the architectural designs promoted by Stickley and his followers anticipate the work of the Prairie School of architects. Published in *The Craftsman* in 1909 and reprinted in *Craftsman Homes*, a book issued the same year, is this classic example of a California house built along the lines of a bungalow. The building is much larger, of course, than the usual rustic bungalow and strongly resembles the work of brothers Charles S. Greene and Henry M. Greene. But in its flowing horizontal profile; use of porches, balconies, and shingling; and the straightforward treatment of framing members, the house is

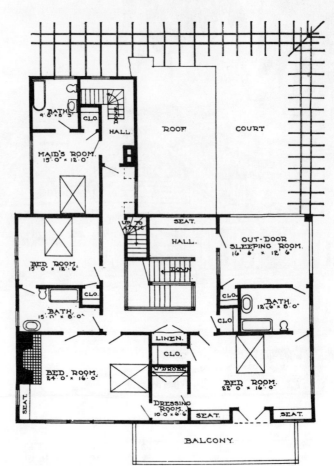

illustrative of contemporary cottage or bungalow architecture. The whole building is hugged by a gradually sloping and overhanging roof; three sides of the house are enclosed by porches. The arrangement of rooms and adjacent outdoor living areas suggests an informal life style which suits the California climate but would also be suitable for other warm areas of North America. This was considered a "California" house when published, and, within a decade or two, it would be copied in various proportions and combinations of elements in all areas of the United States. A living room with a fireplace nook and window seats, a kitchen with a breakfast nook, an outdoor dining area—these and other features were soon to become commonplace in cottage architecture.

Cottages of one or one-and-a-half stories received special attention from architects in the 1920s and '30s. These were affordable homes for the average middle-class family and were built by the hundreds of thousands. The bungalow was one of the popular forms of cottage architecture, an elongated rectangle which would fit easily on a narrow, inexpensive lot. The building was often two rooms wide and two or three deep, and it might also include an attic floor that could be used for storage or additional sleeping space. Many bungalows were built with a porch over the entire front, while others, like the design illustrated here from *Small Homes of Architectural Distinction* (1929), display only a side entryway. This bungalow gains its special picturesque quality from the use of half-timbering in the front gable. Inside, there is another special feature—the placement of the kitchen at the front. "Considering how much time the housewife spends in this room," the architects wrote, "is it not proper that it be given an interesting outlook?" This arrangement enabled the bedrooms to be placed at the rear, allowing for "greater quiet and privacy."

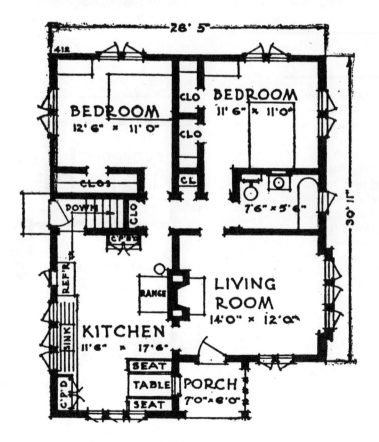

FIRST-FLOOR PLAN.

Termed a bungalow by the
editors of *Small Homes of
Architectural Distinction*, this
wood frame house more
closely resembles an old-
fashioned cottage. Rather than
a low-pitched roof, it has a
steep roof that could allow for
more than attic storage space.
The essential living space,
however, is encompassed on
the first floor. There are two
bedrooms at the rear, and at
the front, as in the previous
design, is situated the kitchen
and living room. And, as in
the other design, there is a
breakfast nook. To have this
facing the front yard and the
street or road was, at that
time, considered an
advantage.

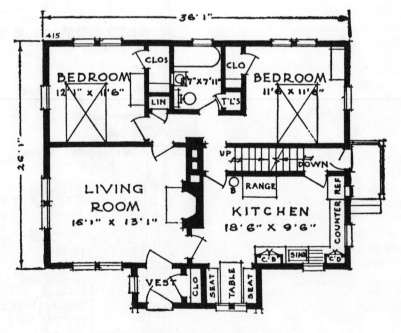

FLOOR PLAN.

The long sloping roof
intersected by a double
dormer and the recessed
porch mark this house as
being classically bungaloid.
Robert L. Stevenson, the
architect and author of
Homes of Character (1923),
pointed out that this narrow
building—22′ feet wide—was
ideal for a small town lot. The
rooms are small, but there is
provision for all basics: a
kitchen with attached pantry
and space for an icebox, plen-
ty of closet space in the
bedrooms, and a full bath.
Excluding the porch, there is
570 square feet of living
space.

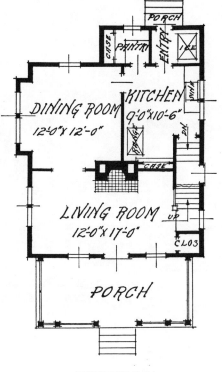

FIRST-FLOOR PLAN.

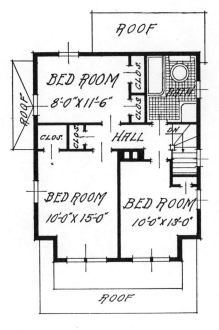

SECOND-FLOOR PLAN.

Stevenson's design for a larger bungalow also makes room for an attached garage at the rear. "To the man building a home of moderate cost," he explained, "this close proximity of his garage is of advantage in that it places his car at his immediate disposal and the garage is more readily heated." In the 1920s, the thought of housing more than one car occurred to few. The one car was "his" car. This house is wider—28'—than the bungalow on page 77 and includes a living area of 1,032 square feet, exclusive of garage and porch. There is still only one bath—located on the second floor. Both the dining room and living room are fitted with fireplaces, and there is provision for a kitchen flue to vent a coal or wood range. Unlike most cottages or bungalows, the construction is brick rather than frame.

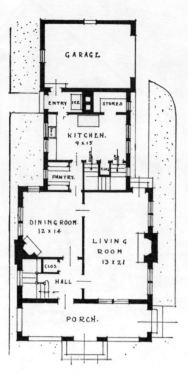

FIRST-FLOOR PLAN.

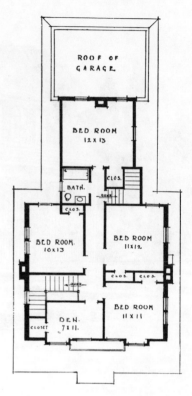

SECOND-FLOOR PLAN.

CORNER ELEVATION.

A stucco-finished wood frame bungalow published in *Small Homes of Architectural Distinction* has the narrow, extended form suited to a small lot. There is only one story, the bedrooms being located in the rear section away from street noise. A recessed side porch serves as a fair-weather living room. The architect has also included a breakfast nook off the kitchen. As the floor plan shows, the house is built above a basement.

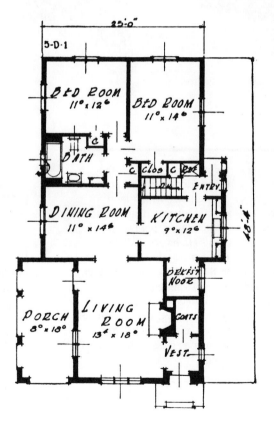

GROUND-FLOOR PLAN.

A cottage designed along the lines of an English Tudor manor house features a high-ceilinged living room and great window. Of frame and brick construction, the building is partially stuccoed. The massive brick chimney, heavy wooden beams exposed over the windows, and half-timbers of the front gable add stylistic character to the exterior. Inside, there are several elements such as the fireplace inglenook in the living room and kitchen dining nook which lend special interest. The architect of this design published in *Small Homes of Architectural Distinction* takes special pride in the kitchen, "replete with space-saving equipment scientifically arranged." The bedrooms and bath have been placed at one side of the cottage as if in a separate wing.

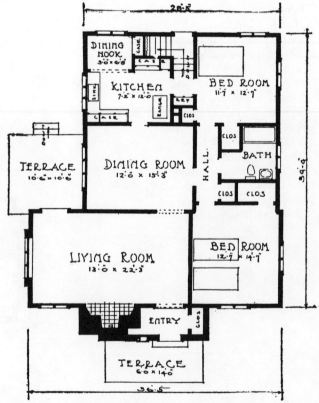

FLOOR PLAN.

With a convenient attached garage and a more extensive floor plan than the usual bungalow, this six-room house is built in two sections. The front rectangle contains a large living room (14' x 22'), dining room, kitchen, and entry hall with coat closet. A variation on this plan, one that would include a breakfast nook, is also shown. Behind the main section are two bedrooms and a large bath with linen closet. The attic floor could also be used for bedrooms, but no plan is provided in *Small Homes of Architectural Distinction*.

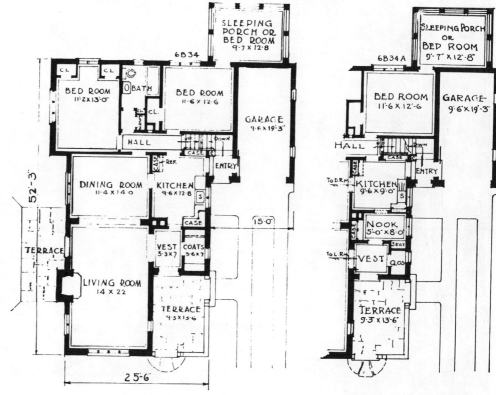

6B34

SLEEPING PORCH OR BED ROOM
9'-7" x 12'-8"

BED ROOM
11'-2 x 13'-0"

CL   CL

BATH

BED ROOM
11'-6 x 12'-6

CL   CL

GARAGE
9'-6 x 19'-3"

HALL

DOWN

CASE

REF.

ENTRY

DINING ROOM
11'-4 x 14'-0

KITCHEN
9'-6 x 12'-8

S

52'-3"

CASE

15'-0"

TERRACE

VEST
5'-3 x 7

COATS
3'-6 x 7

LIVING ROOM
14 x 22

TERRACE
9'-5 x 13'-6

25'-6"

FLOOR PLAN.

6B34A

SLEEPING PORCH OR BED ROOM
9'-7" x 12'-8"

BED ROOM
11'-6 x 12'-6

GARAGE
9'-6 x 19'-3"

HALL

DOWN

CASE

TO D.RM.

KITCHEN
9'-6 x 9'-0"

S

ENTRY

CASE

NOOK
5'-0" x 8'-0

SEAT

TO L.RM.

VEST

CLOS.

TERRACE
9'-3 x 13'-6"

ALTERNATIVE FLOOR PLAN OF RIGHT SECTION OF HOUSE.

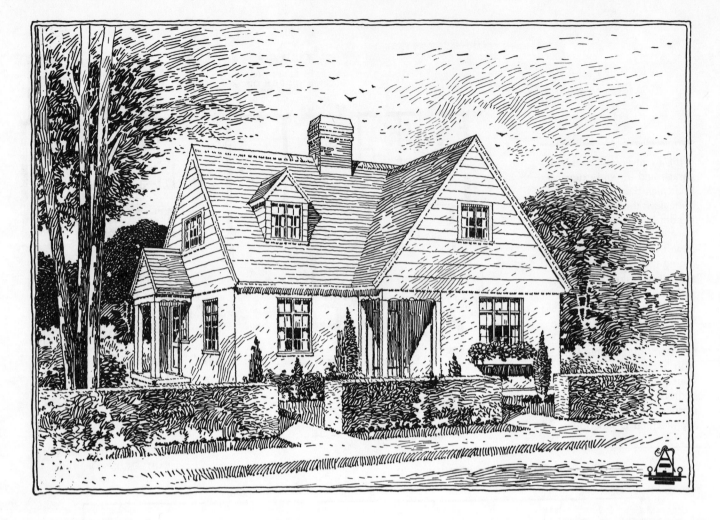

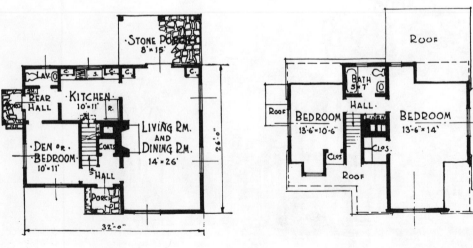

FIRST-FLOOR PLAN.

SECOND-FLOOR PLAN.

If it were not for the front gable extension, this small cottage would have the lines of a boxy Colonial-style house. The architects, writing in *Small Homes of Distinction,* call the style ''English.'' Construction is wood frame throughout, with a stucco finish on the first floor and rough siding of random widths on the upper story. The basic plan is modest and flexible, with a living room that could also be used for dining, a den or bedroom, and both rear and front halls. The lavatory on the first floor is a special convenience, and useful for anyone occupying a first-floor bedroom.

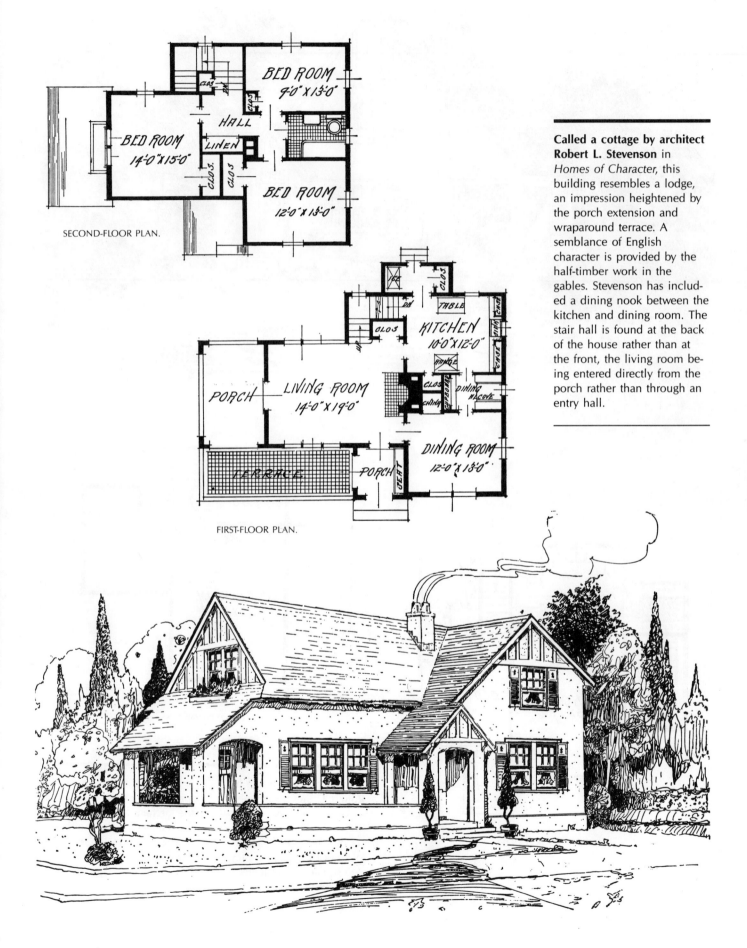

SECOND-FLOOR PLAN.

BED ROOM
9'-0" X 13'-0"

HALL

LINEN

BED ROOM
14'-0" X 15'-0"

CLOS.

CLOS

CLOS

BED ROOM
12'-0" X 13'-0"

CLOS

TABLE

KITCHEN
10'-0" X 12'-0"

RANGE

CLOS

DINING ALCOVE

CHINA

PORCH

LIVING ROOM
14'-0" X 19'-0"

TERRACE

PORCH

SEAT

DINING ROOM
12'-0" X 13'-0"

FIRST-FLOOR PLAN.

Called a cottage by architect Robert L. Stevenson in *Homes of Character*, this building resembles a lodge, an impression heightened by the porch extension and wraparound terrace. A semblance of English character is provided by the half-timber work in the gables. Stevenson has included a dining nook between the kitchen and dining room. The stair hall is found at the back of the house rather than at the front, the living room being entered directly from the porch rather than through an entry hall.

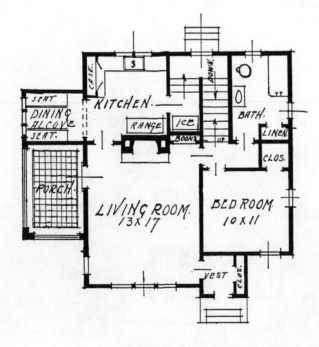

FIRST-FLOOR PLAN.

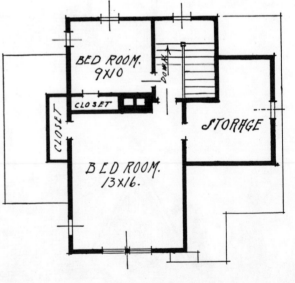

SECOND-FLOOR PLAN.

A small cottage design by Robert L. Stevenson only lacks the necessary gingerbread to take its place on the set of *Hansel and Gretel*. Without the porch, it provides 700 square feet of living space on two full levels. There is no dining room; an alcove for this purpose is situated off the kitchen. In the words of the architect, "The interior is arranged to give the maximum comfort in a house of this size."

Another cottage designed by Stevenson has even fewer rooms than the previous design—four rather than five—but these are better proportioned. The total living space—all on one convenient floor—covers 915 square feet rather than 700. There is a vestibule through which one enters the house, and just inside the living room is a fireplace alcove. A second alcove off the kitchen and living room serves as a dining nook. Two bedrooms are divided by a bathroom. Closets are in good supply, and the attic floor could also be used for storage.

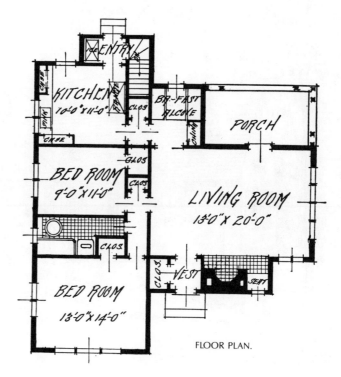

FLOOR PLAN.

Called a bungalow by architect Robert L. Stevenson, this small building is not unlike many wood-frame cottages built in the 20th century. Its only distinction is the wide front porch with half-timber gable and the building's stucco finish. A rectangle divided into four sections, the cottage contains the bare minimum of amenities in 876 square feet of space. The place of a dining room is taken by an alcove extension.

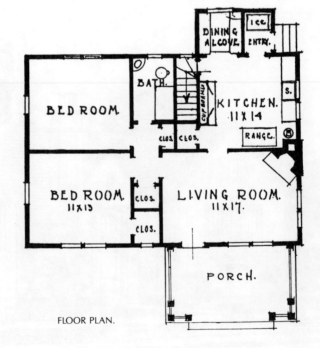

FLOOR PLAN.

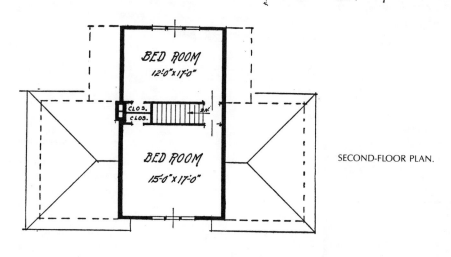

BED ROOM
12'-0"x17'-0"

CLOS.
CLOS.

BED ROOM
15'-0"x17'-0"

SECOND-FLOOR PLAN.

Another cottage design by Robert L. Stevenson is unusual for its broad proportions. Forty-six-feet wide, the building is centered on a large front hall, another unusual feature for a cottage. Fieldstone is used as the building material for the first floor; the second story is wood frame that has been stuccoed with half-timbers. The master bedroom is found on the first floor with an adjoining bath. Two other bedrooms are tucked into the center of the second-story space.

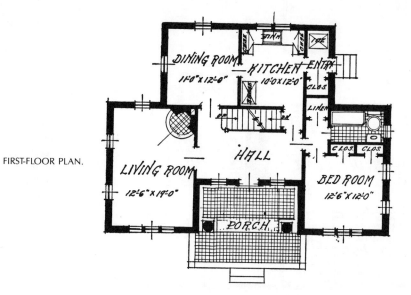

FIRST-FLOOR PLAN.

DINING ROOM
11'-0"x12'-0"

KITCHEN
10'-0"x12'-0"

ENTRY

CLOS

LINEN

CLOS CLOS

HALL

LIVING ROOM
12'-6"x19'-0"

BED ROOM
12'-6"x12'-0"

PORCH

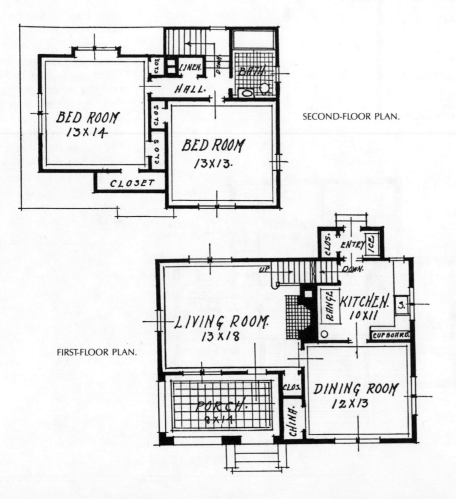

SECOND-FLOOR PLAN.

BED ROOM 13X14

CLOS.

LINEN.

DOWN

BATH

HALL.

CLOS.

CLOS.

BED ROOM 13X13.

CLOSET

FIRST-FLOOR PLAN.

CLOS.

ENTRY

CL.

UP

DOWN.

RANGE

KITCHEN. 10X11

J.

LIVING ROOM. 13X18

CUPBOARD.

PORCH. 8X14

CLOS.

CHINA.

DINING ROOM 12X13

Robert L. Stevenson won first prize in a competition for a small house of five rooms conducted by the Building Trade Employers Association of New York in the early 1900s. Overall there is only 704 square feet of living space in his prize-winning entry, but this is imaginatively divided. The recessed front porch serves as an entry hall to the living room and, in the architect's words, "can readily be enclosed for a sun porch at small additional expense." All the rooms are well equipped with storage space, the dining room having its own built-in china closet. The house is built of wood frame with a stucco finish.

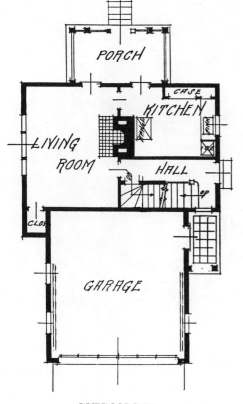

FIRST-FLOOR PLAN.

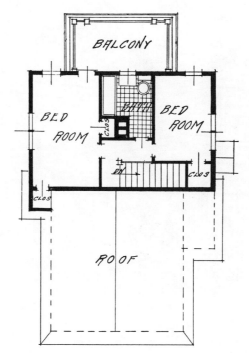

SECOND-FLOOR PLAN.

Hillside cottages continued to be built in the early 1900s, although it was becoming easy to transform a steep building site with mechanized earthmoving equipment. This cottage was designed to serve two purposes—as a garage and chauffeur's dwelling place. The two-car garage is completely separated from the apartment by a fire wall. As befits a building on an estate, architect Stevenson has dressed the gables with half-timbers and the wood frame walls with a stucco finish. An old-fashioned door hood protects the side entry to the house.

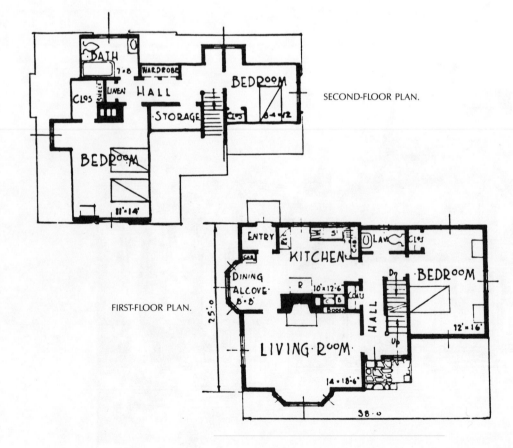

SECOND-FLOOR PLAN.

FIRST-FLOOR PLAN.

Bay windows are the special feature of this five-room cottage design from *Small Homes of Architectural Distinction*. One serves as a dining alcove off the kitchen, and the second provides a graceful niche in the living room which could be fitted with a window seat. The rustic character of the cottage is enhanced by the use of rough siding on the gable ends and a stucco finish on the first floor. The roof overhangs the front and back of the house and gives the building a protected, sheltered appearance. Inside, halls on each floor provide access to all rooms, thereby eliminating the need to pass through one room to reach another. Note the placement of a small lavatory on the first floor and a larger bathroom on the second.

A four-room one-story bungalow designed by Robert L. Stevenson contains an expansive 1,020 square feet of living space. With only one bedroom, however, it is only appropriate for one person or a couple. The enclosed sun porch could presumably serve as a bedroom as well, but it is not positioned well for this purpose. The elevation shows a stucco finish, but the architect suggested that shingles or clapboards would be just as appropriate.

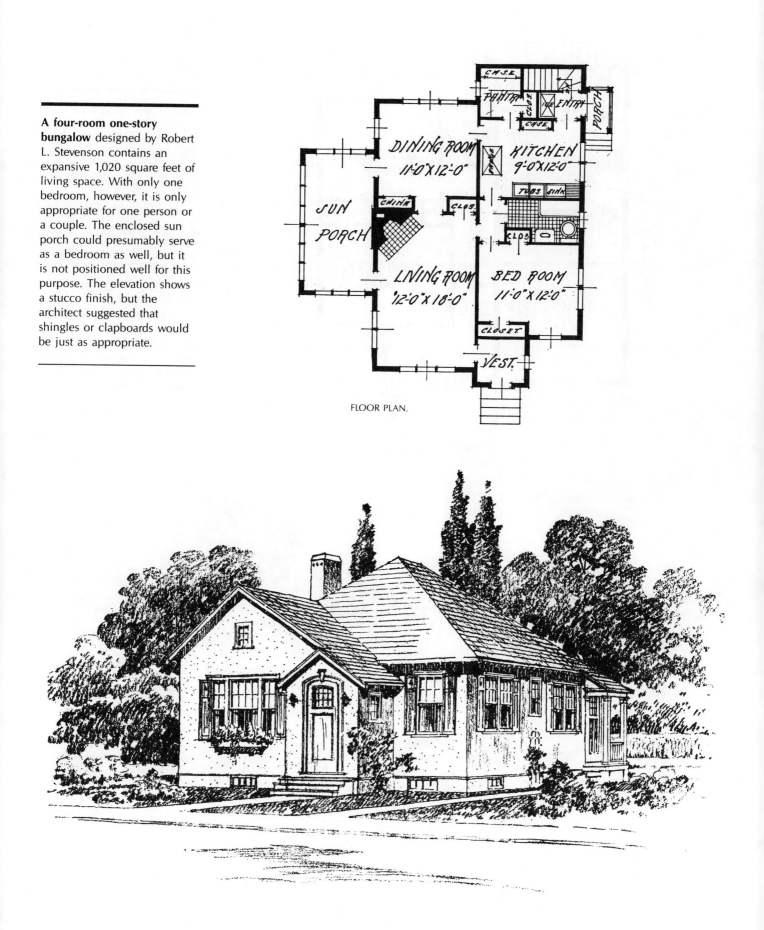

FLOOR PLAN.

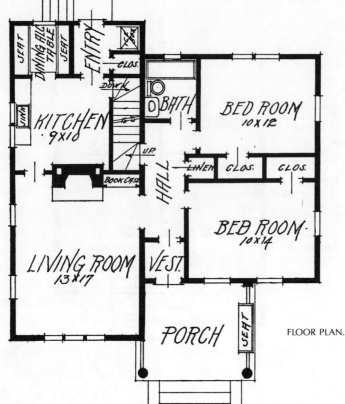

FLOOR PLAN.

Similar in style to the bungalow on page 91 is this four-room cottage. It provides two bedrooms and a kitchen and living room that are slightly smaller; the dining room has been eliminated, a dining area added in its place to the kitchen. A center hall neatly divides sleeping space from the other rooms. The second floor is of great enough height to allow for the addition of bedrooms, the dormer and gable windows providing light and air. This design is also by Robert Stevenson and, as in many of his plans, a stucco finish is used for the exterior walls.

Economy was uppermost in the mind of the designer of this five-room cottage featured in *Small Homes of Architectural Distinction.* Built of texture face hollow tile, it requires no finish as these tiles were then available in a variety of colors and textures. A blockhouse, one might call it, but the architect has included such features as double-hung sash divided not into one solid piece of glass each but into six lights. The latticework porch also helps to soften the crude lines of the building. Inside, there is similar good planning. A back hall functionally divides the bedrooms from the front living room, kitchen, and dining room. The kitchen can be entered from a separate side entrance.

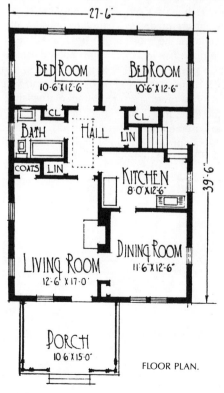

FLOOR PLAN.

A neat four-room brick cottage is also a very economical one to build. The design from *Small Houses of Architectural Distinction* is similar to that used later in small ranch-style homes. Considerable savings are made by eliminating ceilings; the roof serves double duty. The lack of ceilings also gives the small rooms a much more spacious appearance. Unlike most cottages of the time, this house has no basement and only a concrete floor laid over the ground and finished with linoleum. The architect explains that in order to eliminate any dampness, the concrete flooring is laid over ten inches of loose rock topped with gravel. The sectional drawing shows yet another unusual feature for the time: a dormer which, when open during warm months, helps to keep the house cool, and when closed during cold weather, keeps heat from escaping. The design was published in *Small Homes of Architectural Distinction.*

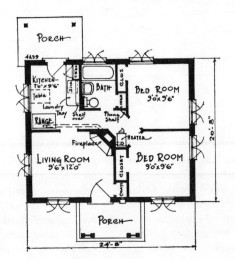

FLOOR PLAN.

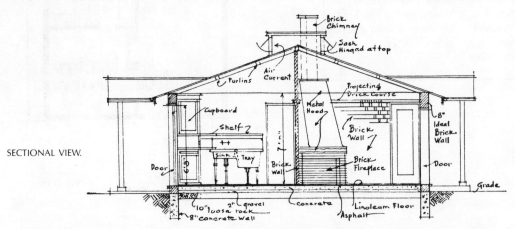

SECTIONAL VIEW.

Very similar to the cottage shown on page 93 is this building also built of structural tile and presented in *Small Homes of Architectural Distinction*. It is slightly smaller than the previous cottage and somewhat less expensive to build. There is no fireplace and, rather than a dining room, a dining alcove is located between the living room and kitchen. The bedrooms are segregated on one side of the house with a full bath in between; a hall connecting the two bedrooms also contains space for a linen closet and a coat closet.

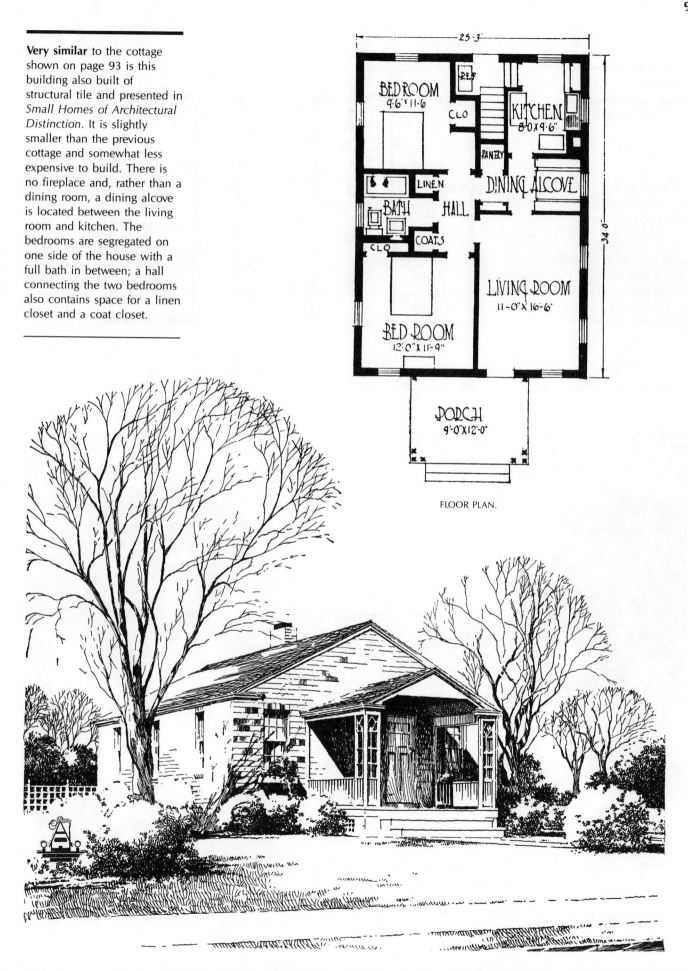

FLOOR PLAN.

Designed for a family needing four bedrooms and published in *Small Homes of Architectural Distinction*, this bungalow is also built of texture face hollow tile. A dining room is eliminated to make room for two bedrooms on the first floor; two additional rooms run back to back on the second floor. The architect was particularly proud of the small but well-arranged kitchen which included a sink, "placed beneath a double window [which] affords an outlook over the yard and garden," and such built-in features as an ironing board and cabinet.

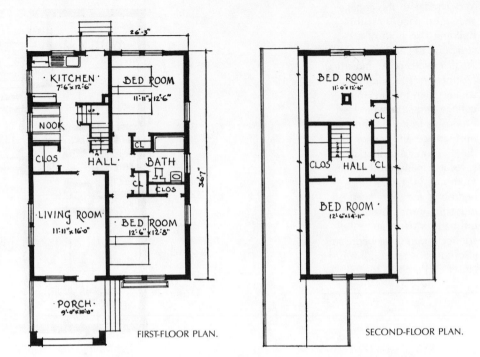

FIRST-FLOOR PLAN.

SECOND-FLOOR PLAN.

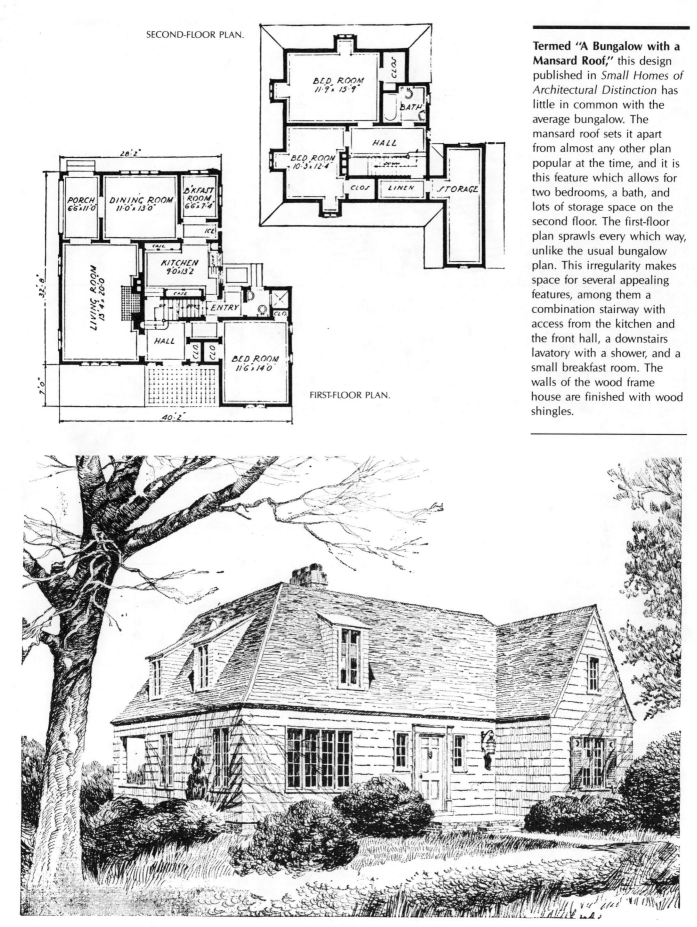

SECOND-FLOOR PLAN.

BED ROOM
11'·9" x 15'·9"

CLO.

BATH

HALL

BED ROOM
10'·3" x 12'·4"

CLOS

LINEN

STORAGE

28'·2"

PORCH
6'·6" x 11'·0"

DINING ROOM
11'·0" x 13'·0"

B'K'FAST
ROOM
6'·6" x 7'·4"

ICE

32'·8"

LIVING ROOM
13'·4" x 20'·0"

CEIL.

KITCHEN
9'·0" x 13'·2"

CEIL.

ENTRY

CLO.

HALL

UP DN

CLO

CLO

BED ROOM
11'·6" x 14'·0"

7'·0"

40'·2"

FIRST-FLOOR PLAN.

Termed "A Bungalow with a Mansard Roof," this design published in *Small Homes of Architectural Distinction* has little in common with the average bungalow. The mansard roof sets it apart from almost any other plan popular at the time, and it is this feature which allows for two bedrooms, a bath, and lots of storage space on the second floor. The first-floor plan sprawls every which way, unlike the usual bungalow plan. This irregularity makes space for several appealing features, among them a combination stairway with access from the kitchen and the front hall, a downstairs lavatory with a shower, and a small breakfast room. The walls of the wood frame house are finished with wood shingles.

This five-room design
encompasses all the basic
needs of a small family on
one floor. The second floor
was intended for storage only,
although the designer, writing
in *Small Homes of
Architectural Distinction*,
claimed enough headroom
was provided here for adding
two more bedrooms at a later
date. A stairway is positioned
in the middle of the house
and provides convenient
access to the basement or
second floor. There is both a
front and back porch.
Casement windows are used
rather than double-hung sash
and give the house a
distinctive look.

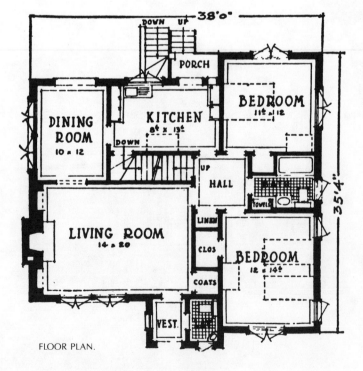

FLOOR PLAN.

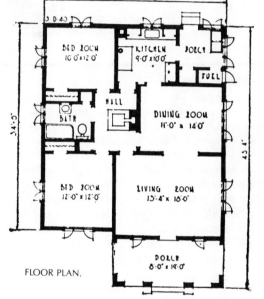

FLOOR PLAN.

Spanish Colonial or Mission-style bungalows with stuccoed walls and tile roofs gained great popularity in the 1920s. Although best suited for a reasonably warm climate such as California or the Deep South, buildings of this type were constructed throughout the United States. Those not requiring a central heating system, however, could be built without a basement necessary for housing a coal-burning furnace. Both bungalows shown here, published in *Small Homes of Architectural Distinction*, were intended for the Sun Belt. The floor plan is virtually the same for both, as one building differs in form from the other mainly in its orientation on the site. The bungalow with the porch on the front makes use of casement windows; that with the side porch uses more common double-hung sash. Either house, the architect claimed, could be built for less than $4,500 in 1929.

100

Two additional cellarless bungalow designs were presented in *Small Homes of Architectural Distinction*, where it was claimed that eliminating a basement could save a homeowner as much as fifteen percent of his building costs. The same floor plan serves both houses. One bungalow, because of a stucco finish and tile roof, is Spanish Colonial in style; the other, with wide clapboards and shingled roof, is closer to an English Colonial model. There is a space in each for what was called a "heating plant"; this is marked on the floor plan as "fuel." "There are on the market various forms of ground floor heaters," it was explained, "which heat five or six rooms comfortably."

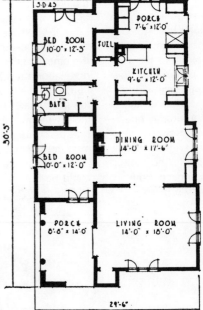

GROUND-FLOOR PLAN.

A cottage in the Mission style, published in *Small Houses of Architectural Distinction*, is built of hollow tile and stuccoed. With the addition of a tile roof, side balcony, arched door and window openings, and a recessed porch, the romantic quality of this small house is established. The architect has included two full baths, an unusual feature in a cottage measuring 28′ x 36′, and an exceptionally large living room. The dining room has been cut back to alcove size.

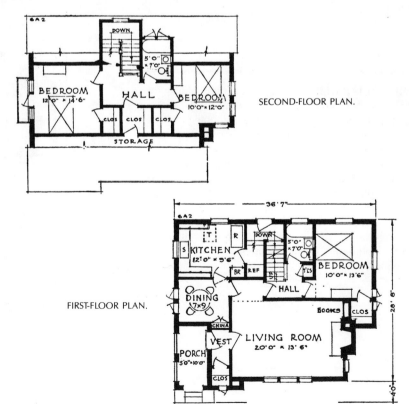

SECOND-FLOOR PLAN.

FIRST-FLOOR PLAN.

Concrete walls, finished with stucco, enclose this bungalow "in the California manner." The main entrance is a bit confusing, leading to both the kitchen and living room, but the dining room which opens up to a patio is a pleasant feature. The patio can also be reached through French doors at one side of the living room. Two small bedrooms are in a rear wing of the U-shaped building. Oddly for a building of this style, the windows are double-hung sash rather than casement. Although designed primarily for the Sun Belt, this model was also recommended by the writer in *Small Homes of Architectural Distinction* as a house "for more rigorous climates." The house includes a basement.

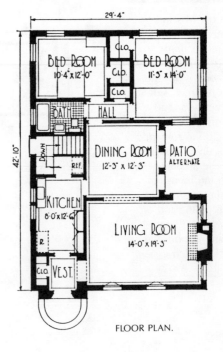

FLOOR PLAN.

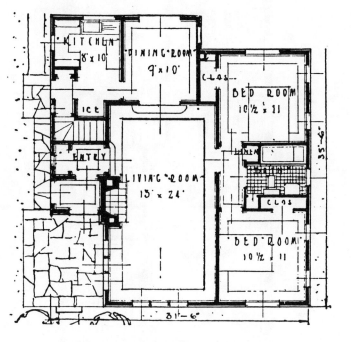

FLOOR PLAN.

Anyone tired of what the architect called "the average commonplace shoebox bungalow" would delight in this very different design for a Mission-style bungalow published in *Small Homes of Architectural Distinction*. The extended living room is situated several feet below the level of the entry, as are also the side bedrooms and bath. The dropped living room is called a "studio" and enjoys a raised ceiling and triple windows extending nearly two floors at one end of the room. The kitchen and dining room are on the same higher level as the entry. This building is not of concrete construction but frame with a stucco finish. The roof is shingled, but could just as well be tiled. In keeping with the California style, the windows are casement.

Called a "bungalow apartment" in *Small Homes of Architectural Distinction,* this small house is intended for those who want "a house with the conveniences of the apartment." The walls are composed of concrete blocks faced with stucco, an economical alternative to wood-frame construction. Cast stone trim is used around the windows and doorways; an ornamental chimney cap and molded ornaments are placed elsewhere on the exterior to give the building a picturesque, romantic character. Floors are reinforced concrete over which linoleum has been laid.

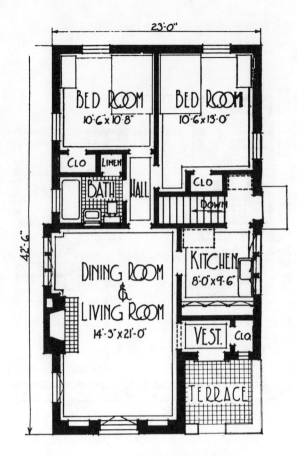

FLOOR PLAN.

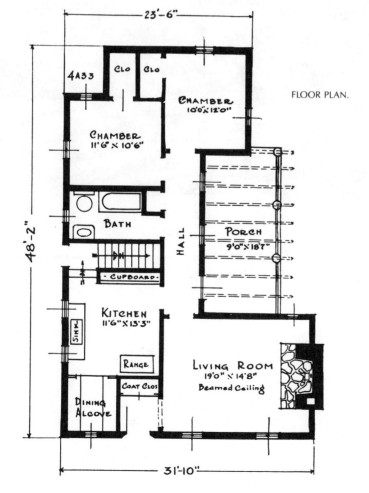

FLOOR PLAN.

A precursor of the ranch-
style house of the 1950s is
what was termed a Spanish
Colonial cottage in the 1920s.
Published in *Small Homes of
Architectural Distinction*, the
building centers on a long
front porch or verandah from
which one enters a long hall.
Living room and kitchen, with
dining alcove, are situated in
one wing, the bath in the
middle, and two bedrooms in
the opposite wing. ''The
bedrooms,'' the designer
notes, ''have almost the
privacy of a separate
apartment.'' The living room
is very well appointed with a
beamed ceiling, casement
windows that reach to the
floor, and a massive stone
fireplace.

The same basic floor plan is used for both these cottages, one Spanish Colonial in style and the other, on the opposite page, a vernacular building with some English Colonial details. The writer in *Small Homes of Architectural Distinction* suggests that either house might be positioned with the narrow side toward the street, thus making it suitable for a narrow lot. In that case, the open entry porch would be moved to what was the side. As in other designs interpreted in these two styles, the walls and roofs are finished in different ways: one building employs casement windows; and the other, double-hung sash.

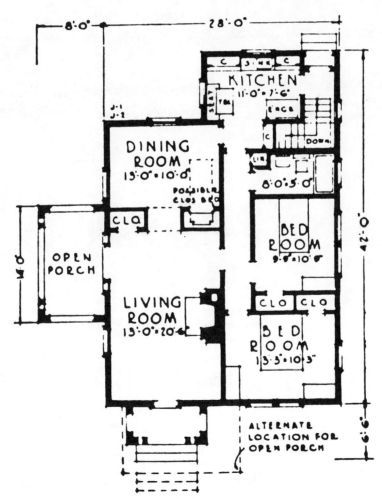

FLOOR PLAN.

Although simple in construction and small in size, this four-room bungalow in the Mission style has a sophisticated apperance, created by the use of an arched porch with wrought-iron railings, sculpted gables, and an almost flat roof. The walls are built of hollow tile and then finished with stucco. A basement underlies part of the house and provides room for a laundry, furnace room, and fuel storage room, thus making the building suitable for either a warm or cold climate. The bedrooms are arranged off a side hall with privacy in mind. The design is from *Small Homes of Architectural Distinction.*

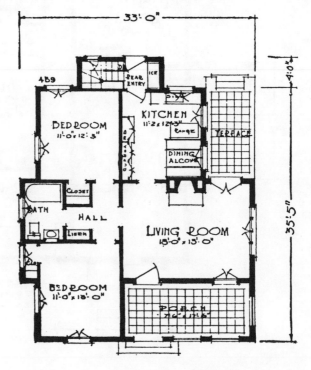

FLOOR PLAN.

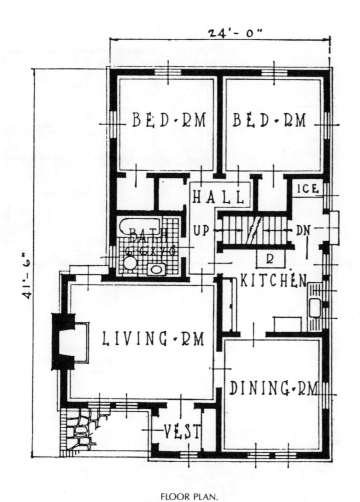

24'- 0"

41'- 6"

BED·RM   BED·RM

HALL   ICE

BATH   UP   DN
6'-6"X 7'6

KITCHEN

LIVING·RM

DINING·RM

VEST

FLOOR PLAN.

What the writer in *Small Homes of Architectural Distinction* termed an American bungalow we would now call a Colonial-style cottage. The saltbox shape of the main part of the house sets the style. Shingles for the exterior finish reinforce the picturesque period appearance. The floor plan is nearly as compact as that found in an early American house, but there is provision here for every modern convenience.

110

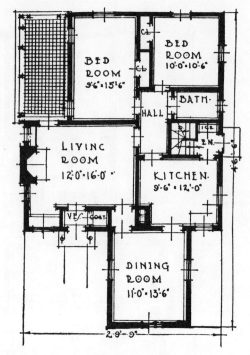

FLOOR PLAN.

A cottage design published in *Small Homes of Architectural Distinction* is termed "demure and friendly" by the writer. Today we would call the style "early American," a vernacular reworking of the classic New England Colonial cottage. Such details as a Palladian window and a front entrance with a transom contribute to the cozy, period feeling. It is unusual to see so much space and attention given to a dining room in a cottage; the architect suggests that the room might be used, instead, as a library or study. Exposed to light on three sides, it is a very airy, pleasant room. The bedrooms at the rear are also well positioned to receive light and cross-ventilation. A special feature of the compact living room is a large fireplace and a corner alcove with window seats.

A little square cottage with
front stoop, seat, and door
hood would be called a
''starter'' or a retirement home
today. As laid out, it is barely
large enough for a modern
couple. The writer in *Small
Homes of Architectural
Distinction* did note, however,
that another bedroom could
be fitted into the attic floor.
The chimney does not serve a
fireplace but, rather, carries a
furnace flue. One of the most
pleasing features of this
modest design is the roof
overhang on two sides of the
building which shelters the
main story.

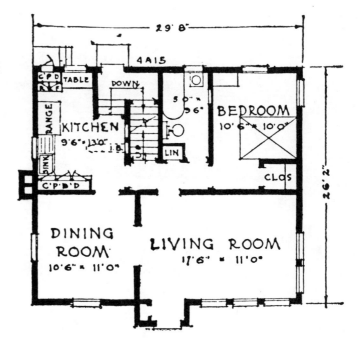

FLOOR PLAN.

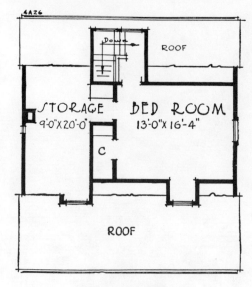

SECOND-FLOOR PLAN.

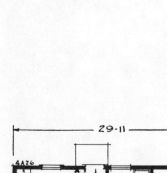

FIRST-FLOOR PLAN.

A design similar to that shown on page 111 is also from *Small Homes of Architectural Distinction*. The roof has flaring eaves which, at the front, enclose a verandah or porch. There are two bedrooms, one on the first floor and the other above. As in the previous cottage, there is no provision for a fireplace.

4A26

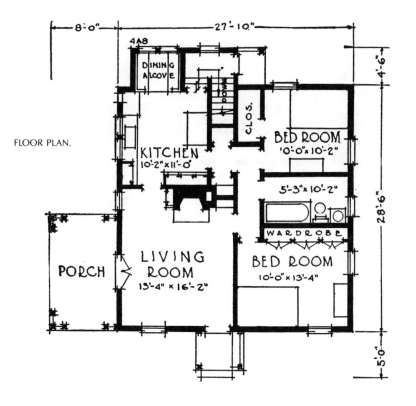

FLOOR PLAN.

The cottage shown here could easily serve as the set for a play about small-town America in the 1920s. Only missing from the porch latticework is a climber rose or flowering vine. The four-room cottage with traditional clapboard siding has as simple a floor plan as there could possibly be. Living room and kitchen are positioned on one side of the house; bedrooms and bath are on the other. Only the extension of the roof and cornice which ties in a side porch is of any visual interest. The design is from *Small Homes of Architectural Distinction.*

Based on a traditional Southern cottage of the mid-1800s, this design from *Small Homes of Architectural Distinction* is reasonably accurate in its exterior detailing. The classic porch is simple and well-proportioned with Ionic columns and a proper cornice. The entryway is suitably made up of sidelights and transom and is suited to the space. The double-hung sash windows are also well-proportioned and distributed. A full basement underlies the whole house, which is raised several feet above ground level. Inside are two bedrooms on one side of the main floor, a large living room with fireplace, and a small kitchen. The architect intended that the attic space be finished off for another bedroom at a later date.

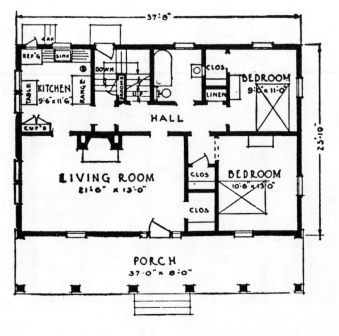

FLOOR PLAN.

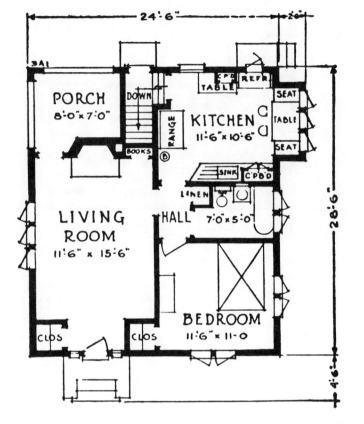

FLOOR PLAN.

A little house measuring approximately 23′ wide and 26′ deep offers a bare minimum of amenities. The rear corner porch could be enclosed to provide a dining room or second bedroom. There is a narrow dining alcove in the kitchen. The entire house is positioned on a full basement where laundry would be done and a furnace and its supply of fuel could be housed The three-room design was published in *Small Homes of Architectural Distinction.*

Another small cottage in
*Small Homes of Architectural
Distinction* is characterized by
a lack of ornament or detail.
The triple-width window
opens up the living room on
one side; a fireplace is the
focus of attention on the other
side of the room. A stair hall
attached to the rear of the
kitchen does not take up any
of the limited floor space.

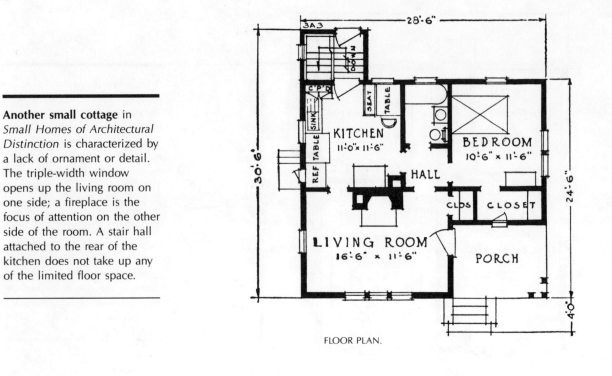

FLOOR PLAN.

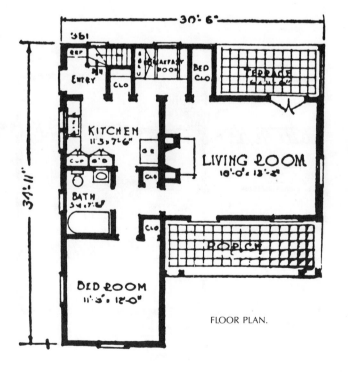

FLOOR PLAN.

A third three-room cottage design published in *Small Homes of Architectural Distinction* has true architectural merit. The size, 30½' x 34' 11"—is only slightly greater than the previous two designs, but the rooms are better proportioned and arranged. The bedroom, because it is thrust out from the main body of the house, has privacy and benefits from cross-ventilation. The good-sized living room is similarly positioned between the front porch and back terrace. A small breakfast nook is provided off the kitchen. Note that the living room has a bed closet at one side. This was a space in which a hideaway bed could be stored until needed at nighttime.

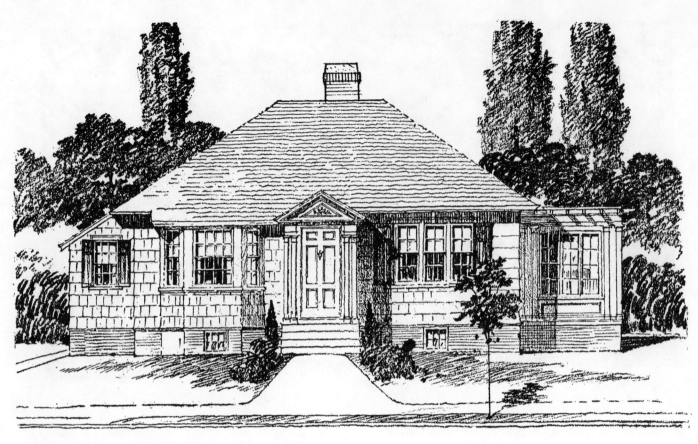

Robert L. Stevenson's design
for a four-room bungalow in
the Colonial style is included
in his book, *Homes of
Character* (1923). The hip roof,
neo-classical vestibule porch,
and shingle siding give the
building its principal
character. The dining room
and living room flow almost
freely into each other and
create a space approximately
12' x 30'. To one side is a sun
porch that could be enclosed
at a later date to form another
bedroom; on the other side of
the house is a stair hall, rear
entry, and bed closet or
dressing room. In the bed
closet Stevenson planned to
store a chiffonier and
moveable bed. At night, the
bed would be moved into the
dining room. A window in
the bed closet ventilates
bedding when not in use.

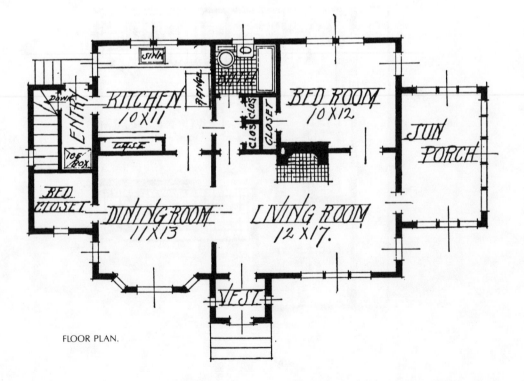

FLOOR PLAN.

FLOOR PLAN.

PORCH

ICE

ENTRY

CASE

CASE

STAIR

CASE

KITCHEN
9'-0" X 12'-0"

RANGE

DINING ROOM
11'-0" X 12'-0"

TERRACE.

LIVING ROOM
14'0" X 18'-0"

PORCH

BED ROOM
11'-0" X 12'-0"

HALL

CLOS

BATH

CLOS   CLOS

BED ROOM
11'0" X 12'-0"

A Stevenson design for a five-room bungalow is better suited for family use. Two bedrooms and a bath are clearly separated from the other principal rooms. The kitchen and dining room flow naturally into each other. A commodious living room is positioned between the front porch and a back terrace. All rooms have good cross ventilation.

A bungalow for a narrow 50' lot was designed by Robert L. Stevenson with a picturesque shingle finish. He proposed two different floor plans, one with an entry hall or vestibule and the second with direct entry from a front porch to the living room. Other important differences are in the position of the stairs to the basement and second floor, the placement of the bath, and inclusion of a den. The elevation shows the exterior features of floor plan A. For the most part, floor plan B is a great deal more logical and is probably less costly in execution.

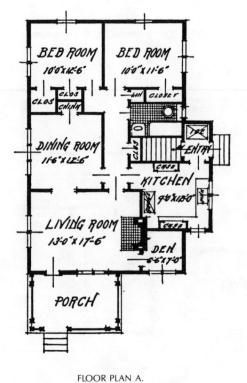

FLOOR PLAN A.

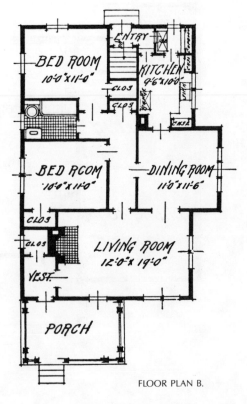

FLOOR PLAN B.

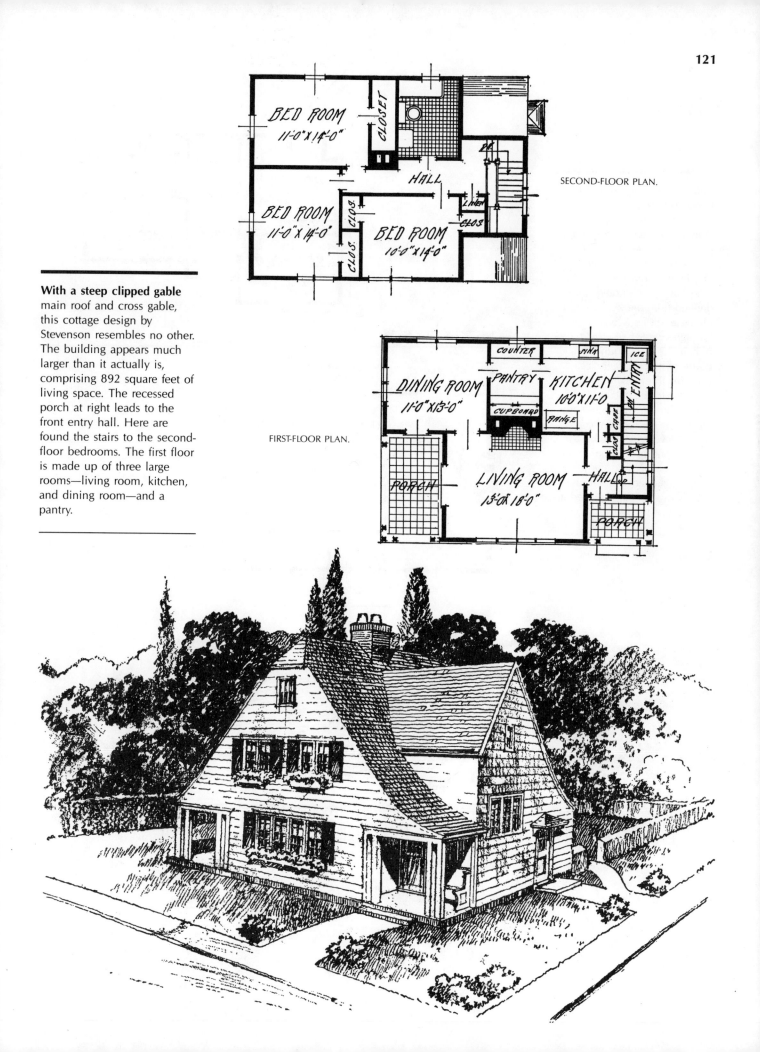

SECOND-FLOOR PLAN.

BED ROOM 11'-0"x14'-0"

CLOSET

HALL

BED ROOM 11'-0"x14'-0"

CLOS.

CLOS.

BED ROOM 10'-0"x14'-0"

LINEN

CLOS

With a steep clipped gable main roof and cross gable, this cottage design by Stevenson resembles no other. The building appears much larger than it actually is, comprising 892 square feet of living space. The recessed porch at right leads to the front entry hall. Here are found the stairs to the second-floor bedrooms. The first floor is made up of three large rooms—living room, kitchen, and dining room—and a pantry.

FIRST-FLOOR PLAN.

COUNTER

SINK

ICE

DINING ROOM 11'-0"x13'-0"

PANTRY

KITCHEN 10'-0"x11'-0"

ENTRY

CUPBOARD

RANGE

CLOS CLOS.

PORCH

LIVING ROOM 13'-0"x18'-0"

HALL

PORCH

Called by Stevenson a "little Colonial cottage," this house of six rooms is unusually compact; excluding the sun porch, there are only 704 square feet of living space. The living room stretches the full depth of the house and is divided from the kitchen and dining room by a floor-through center hall. This type of hall is usually found in a house of much larger size. Upstairs, three bedrooms are tucked into the gables. The one bathroom is conveniently located at the top of the stairs. Stevenson thought it wise to put the sun porch on the rear of the house where it "faces a garden and affords more privacy than if placed at the front of the house."

SECOND-FLOOR PLAN.

BED ROOM
10'-0" X 12'-0"

CLOSET

CLOSET   CLOSET

BED ROOM
10'-0" X 12'-0"

HALL

BED ROOM
9'-0" X 12'-0"

CLOSET

SUN PORCH

ICE ENTRY

DN

LIVING ROOM

CLOS.

CLOS.

UP

KITCHEN
9'-0" X 12'-0"

CASE

SINK

RANGE

12'-0" X 22'-0"

HALL

DINING ROOM
12'-0" X 12'-0"

FIRST-FLOOR PLAN.

PORCH   SEAT

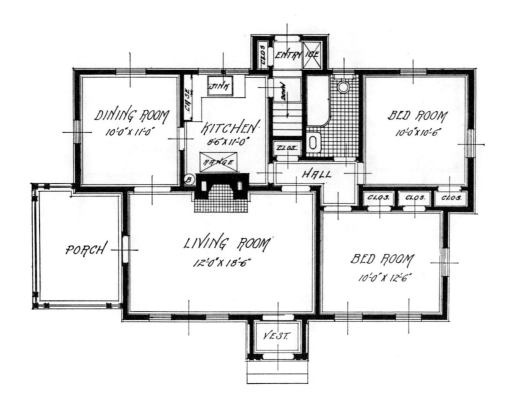

FLOOR PLAN.

A traditional symmetrical Colonial-style cottage was presented by architect Robert Stevenson as the epitome of "great charm." "It is the type of house," he wrote, "that improves with age, as each year it becomes more closely related to its surroundings." Including the side porch, the building is 44' wide; the depth is approximately 25'. Living room, dining room, and kitchen are housed on one side; two bedrooms and a bath are on the other.

A cottage similar in size to the one shown on the previous page has a much larger kitchen and a wide center hall dividing the two bedrooms from the principal rooms. A dining alcove takes the place of the dining room. The entry porch is a wide, comfortably proportioned resting place and not a pretentious facade. Shingles are used for siding, an appropriate choice for a building that depends ''on its simple mass and good proportions for beauty of design.''

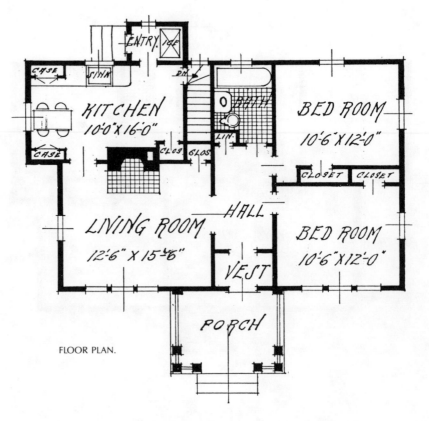

FLOOR PLAN.

Suggested Reading

The literature on popular American cottage architecture is very sparse. Architectural historians have concentrated, instead, on more sophisticated buildings and their architects. Only recently has the importance of published house plans been recognized by academicians. Reprints of some of the influential 19th-century sources of plans are available; other publications must be sought in special library collections.

Allen, Lewis F. *Rural Architecture.* New York: C. M. Saxton, 1852.

The Architects' Small House Service Bureau. *Small Homes of Architectural Distinction.* New York: Harper & Brothers, 1929.

Atwood, Daniel T. *Atwood's Country and Suburban Houses.* New York: Orange, Judd & Co., 1871.

Bicknell, A. J. *Bicknell's Village Builder.* Reprint of the 1872 ed. Watkins Glen, N.Y.: The American Life Foundation & Study Institute, 1976.

_____. *Detail, Cottage and Constructive Architecture.* Reprint of the 1873 ed. Watkins Glen, N.Y.: The American Life Foundation & Study Institute, 1978.

Cleaveland, Henry W., William Backus, and Samuel D. Backus. *Village and Farm Cottages.* New York: D. Appleton and Co., 1856.

Comstock, William T. *Modern Architectural Designs and Details.* Reprint of the 1881 ed. Watkins Glen, N.Y.: The American Life Foundation & Study Institute, 1978.

Downing, A. J. *The Architecture of Country Houses.* Reprint of the 1850 ed. New York: Dover Publications, 1969.

_____. *Cottage Residences.* Reprint of the 1873 ed. New York: Dover Publications, 1981.

Handlin, David. *The American Home: Architecture and Society, 1815-1915.* Boston: Little, Brown and Co., 1979.

Palliser, Palliser & Co. *Palliser's New Cottage Homes and Details.* Reprint of the 1887 ed. Watkins Glen, N.Y.: The American Life Foundation & Study Institute, n.d.

Ranlett, William H. *The Architect.* Vol. 2. New York: Dewitt & Davenport, 1851

Sloan, Samuel. *The Model Architect.* Vols. 1 and 2. Reprint of the 1852 ed. New York: Dover Publications, 1980.

Stevenson, Robert L. *Homes of Character.* Boston: Robert L. Stevenson, 1923.

Stickley, Gustav. *Craftsman Homes.* Reprint of the 1909 ed. New York: Dover Publications, 1979.

Thomas, J. J. *Illustrated Annual Register of Rural Affairs.* Albany, N.Y.: Luther Tucker & Son, 1873.

Vaux, Calvert. *Villages and Cottages.* Reprint of the 1864 ed. New York: Dover Publications, 1970.

Woodward, George E. *Woodward's Architecture and Rural Art.* Nos. 1 and 2. Reprint of the 1867 and 1868 editions. Watkins Glen, N.Y.: The American Life Foundation & Study Institute, 1978.